# DIT[illegible] HIGH STREET AGENT

## SAVE THOUSANDS OF £££S BY SELF-MANAGING YOUR RENTAL PROPERTY

LOUIS BAMBERGER

*www.mxbproperty.com*
*contact@mxbproperty.com*

Helping landlords save money and confidently self-manage their rental properties

## About the Author

Let me start by telling you a little bit about me··· as soon as I've got over the awkwardness of having to write in the third person.

Louis Bamberger (yes, that's me, this feels so weird) bought his first property in 2007 with no intention of becoming a landlord. He wanted to just live in it like a normal person.

However, a move to London to be closer to work meant he started renting out his property, thus becoming an "accidental" landlord. And for the most part, he loved it.

Over the subsequent years, he quickly expanded his portfolio of rental properties after seeing the long-term financial benefits these offered.

Initially using high street agents to manage these properties, he grew frustrated with their ever-growing fees. While he wouldn't want to appear greedy, he did want more money to justify the work he was putting in, so he switched to being a self-managing landlord and hasn't looked back since.

As a tenant himself, he is uniquely positioned to see both sides of property rental—that of a landlord and a tenant. This perspective has allowed him to build a thriving property business while providing good quality, affordable homes for his satisfied tenants to live in.

Louis is a qualified accountant and works full-time in Financial Services in London. He lives with his wife and two young kids in Surrey. He occasionally exercises, enjoys drinking a chilled beverage, and on rare occasions is able to get a full night's sleep.

## Big Fat Disclaimer

It's only fair—and indeed common sense—to add a disclaimer before we get started.

This book provides landlords with the steps required to switch to becoming a self-managing landlord, i.e. "going it alone" without a high street agent. There are many advantages and some disadvantages of making this switch, which will be covered shortly, but only YOU can decide whether it's right for you based on your unique circumstances.

So, use this book as a practical guide, but ultimately, you'll need to make the decision on whether or not to switch, and take responsibility for this yourself. Obvious, right?

What's more, the property rules and regulations are always changing (don't worry, this book tells you how to keep in touch with these changes). The rules that I have summarised in this book are accurate at the time of writing to the best of my best knowledge. However, if in doubt, you should always do your own research or seek professional independent advice.

Finally, I cover the property rental rules and regulations that apply to rental properties in England and Wales. Separate rules exist in Scotland, so these should be independently researched if your rental property is in Scotland.

With that out of the way, let's get on with the book.

# Prologue

Hello, fellow landlords. Reading this book will give you the tools and knowledge to confidently self-manage your rental property, earning you more money, reducing your stress and making you a better and happier landlord.

As a landlord, you'll already know that owning a rental property is a great long-term investment. You benefit from capital gains when house prices rise **AND** earn a source of income when tenants pay you rent. Property investment can significantly increase your wealth, both now and in the future.

Those financial benefits are important to us landlords, which is why most of us do it. But we want more than just financial benefits. We also want a "low touch" rental property—one that requires minimal effort with low stress. In an ideal world, we would have cash (rent) coming into our bank accounts each month without having to spend any time working on our properties.

Does that sound like your current experience of renting out your property? I doubt it··· that's why you are reading this book.

So, why is that not the case? Well, as you'll know, UK residential landlords have been hard hit these last few years. The government has introduced a raft of new costly property rules and punitive tax legislation which have significantly reduced landlords' profits. These profits are further reduced by the downward pressure on rent and struggles to fill properties caused by market uncertainty from Brexit and the COVID-19 crisis.

To make matters worse, traditional high street agents are charging landlords higher fees than ever, while often offering a reduced service, meaning that YOU are having to do more of the agents' work for them, and paying more for that extra work/stress. Not a fair deal.

The tenant fees ban, online competition, and a general consumer move away from high streets means the business model for a high street agent is not as effective as it used to be, and YOU, the landlord, are paying the price for that.

Less money, time-consuming, high stress··· it's no wonder so many landlords are feeling frustrated and questioning whether rental property is worth it anymore. Surely there has to be a better way?

That's how I felt a few years ago as a landlord of 10+ years, having always used high street agents to manage my properties.

I decided it was time to take action and become a self-managing landlord. I could and would do it better.

Even armed with this determination, it was scary. Could I really do a better job than a high street agent? How could I possibly comply with all the rules and regulations? Could I really find a tenant myself? What if I got something wrong? Switching to being a self-managed landlord seemed overwhelming.

I persevered and worked hard to understand all the rules and regulations that apply to property rental by attending property shows, reading property magazines/books and speaking to fellow landlords. Then it was time. I took the leap of faith and started self-managing one of my properties myself.

The transition was a little painful. I'd read books that summarised what rules I needed to comply with, but couldn't find anything that walked me through the practical steps required to make the transition to self-managing. I had to figure this part out by myself. Undeterred, I took notes and learnt from my mistakes. The second property switch was easier. By the third property, I switched to self-managed and I knew the steps and process inside out.

*"All my properties are now self-managed, and I save myself on average £2,500 a year in high street agent fees ON EACH OF MY SIX PROPERTIES. You do the math!"*

I also provide my tenants (I now call them customers, and treat them as such) a great level of service and have put systems in place to reduce time spent, and keep my stress levels low. I'm a happier landlord.

The only thing I question is why I didn't do this years earlier and why I'd ever doubted myself. If only I'd had a guide that walked me through the practical steps in the process, summarising everything I needed to know in one simple place. My bank balance would certainly be much higher. I'd also have more hair on my head.

Well, unlike me, you do have that guide, and it's in your hands right now.

Follow my step-by-step process to confidently switch from using a high street agent to self-managing your property and instantly save yourself THOUSANDS of £££'s every year.

But it's not just more money in your pocket. By following this simple process, you will learn what's involved in running a rental property (and I promise, it's really not hard). It covers all the relevant property rules, along with every practical aspect, such as finding tenants, drafting tenancy agreements and dealing with maintenance issues.

Yet I don't just want to give you the process and teach you the legal requirements. I want you to feel confident on each step of the journey whilst you make this change to self-managed. So, I'll highlight all the worries, unknowns and doubts I encountered on my journey (the "myths" as I now call them), and how each of these can easily be mitigated—the myth busters!

And finally, along the way, I'll share with you all my top landlord tips, gleaned from hours of my own learning from being a tenant myself (yes, I get to see what landlords are like from a tenant' s perspective—a unique insight!) and also from fellow experienced landlords, designed to take your self-managing property rental skills to the next level. Covering areas such as knowing the cost of a void, business mindset and systemisation, you'll quickly become a landlord pro!

The style of this book is deliberately conversational, while following a logical step by step process, making it easy to read and revert back to as/when required. Have fun!

*More money*

*Less stress*

*More knowledgeable*

*Happier*

Sound good? Well, it's time to "Ditch the High Street Agent" and become a self-managing landlord··· the right way.

Louis Bamberger

# Table of Contents

# 1.0 INTRODUCTION

Property is big. It's important. You can't pick up a newspaper, walk along a high street or watch TV without hearing about property.

TV programmes like *Homes Under the Hammer*, *A Place in the Sun*, etc. have even managed to glamorise it. People dream about owning and living in Instagramable (if that's a word!) properties.

And some people (landlords... YOU) know that property is more than just a home to live in. It can be a lucrative investment, offering a range of financial benefits.

Yet for all these financial benefits, life has gotten tougher for landlords. Market conditions, new rules and increased high street agent fees have greatly reduced the profitability of property rental and made it so much harder to run.

A lot of these changes can't be avoided—you have to comply with the law, full stop. But some can be avoided, and should be··· high street agents' fees. Why spend thousands of pounds every year on fees when you can keep your money in your own bank account while offering an improved service to tenants?

I'll show you how that's done in this book. But first, let's take a step back to consider what a landlord is, why we do it, and what the current market has thrown at us—better the devil you know.

*"Since 2018, landlords have seen their profits fall by more than 20%, and in some cases, it has pushed landlords into making a loss."*

## 1.1 What is a Landlord?

The term "landlord" is common enough in day to day life. And it usually comes with negative connotations, with landlords portrayed as ruthless money-grabbing people who force tenants to live in slum accommodation whilst lining their bank balances with inflated rents. Those stereotypes have built up with years of bad press and horror stories.

In the vast majority of cases, those stereotypes are completely wrong. In reality, landlords make up a variety of people from all walks of life. Male or female, old or young, individuals, couples, families or companies. Some own multiple properties and run them as their main source of income, others have just one property. Some know exactly why they are a landlord with specific goals they want to achieve, others kind of "fall" into property rental and don't know where they want to take it.

Yes, some landlords are ruthless money-grabbers, however, most are just trying to make some extra money whilst providing an invaluable service to the UK economy. There really is no typical landlord.

In this book, I'll refer to a "landlord" (YOU) as someone who owns a property/properties that they rent out to someone else (the tenant). Likely with a view of benefitting financially from the arrangement. Specifically, I'll be referring to residential property, which means that tenant lives in the property (i.e. it's their home) rather than a commercial property where the tenant is a business, i.e. a shop. Simple, hey?

So, how many landlords are there in the UK?

According to the latest figures:

*"There are over 2.66 million private-sector landlords. This number is down slightly on previous years, attributed to the recent tax and rule changes which have caused some landlords to sell up. These landlords are estimated to own 1.93 properties each on average."*

That's 5+ million properties that are let by private landlords, and is expected to account for 20% of the population.

All very rough numbers, of course, but even allowing for some margin of error, that's a very high percentage. This shows just how important the role of the private residential landlord is in the wider property market context. Think about it··· us private residential landlords help to house 20% of the UK population. That is a huge "value add" service to the UK economy.

Yet despite playing such a crucial role in the UK housing market, landlords are a frequent target for scorn by the government, media and public. Fortunately, this book will show you ways that you can help change that perception.

The landlords I know are caring people who provide good quality accommodation to tenants at reasonable rents. They are business people who understand the importance of treating customers well to build a strong relationship that benefits both parties in the long term. As landlords, let's show the world what we do and what we believe in.

We can make a positive difference.

## 1.2 Why be a Landlord?

I'll openly admit, being a landlord often gives me sleepless nights. There are days where I lose money or where it feels like the pile of admin tasks just keeps on growing.

So, why on earth do I do it? Why does any landlord do it for that matter? Surely, it's better to just sell up and stick the money in a bank account?

Well, fortunately, worry, risk and admin are not the only things that landlords get to experience. There are actually many positive benefits to owning a rental property that explain why landlords sacrifice their sleep, risk their own money and spend countless hours of their own time.

What are these benefits? To answer that question, I asked some landlord friends to explain in one short sentence why they own an investment property. Here's what they said, including my own response:

*"For long-term investment."*

*"To supplement our state pension in retirement."*

*"Passive income."*

*"Second income stream to diversify."*

*"Pension supplement/earlier retirement."*

*"Long-term financial gain."*

Some fairly consistent answers there. I'd lump all of those into a "financial benefits" category. These landlords are expecting a financial return from their rental properties, either now or in the future. Which makes perfect sense. Wherever you have risk (I'd extend "risk" to also include worry and admin!), you should get return.

**The risk-return relationship:** Generally, the higher the potential return of an investment, the higher the risk.

Sticking all your money in a low-interest savings account is easy and requires minimal effort. But it also won't give you the same financial benefits that owning a rental property can provide (please note, I'm not saying putting money in a bank account is a bad thing!).

Being a landlord might give you a few grey hairs, but those should more than offset the rewards on offer.

Let's break those financial returns down a bit:

In property terms, the financial returns referred to above arise in the form of cash in your bank account, both now and in the future. Specifically:

- **Source of income:** Means you don't need to rely 100% on your employment income, or pension income when you retire—you are diversifying.
- **Passive income:** Property doesn't require a set number of hours like paid employment.
- **Investment:** Can give rise to future capital gains, which can be converted to cash on sale, or passed down to future generations.

What will you do with the rental income and capital gains? That's up to you··· retire earlier, more holidays, less work, better lifestyle? You choose!

Believe it or not, there are even non-financial types of "return" for landlords that can explain why we own a rental property:

- **Property is a people business:** It's enjoyable working with different people.
- **Interest/passion/purpose:** Property can be interesting. It's everywhere we look. It's tangible. It's real. I love it.

- **Helping the community:** Despite what the press might have you believe, as a landlord, you serve an important purpose providing a home in the private rental sector.

So, is it worth it?

**Absolutely**. As landlords, we will on occasion feel worried, be snowed under with admin and can even lose money. But there is (or at least should be) a very good reason you are a landlord.

I'd encourage every landlord to have a quick think about what their reason is. And then every time your property feels stressful or takes up your time, just remember that reason with a smile.

*"For me, the main reason is the long-term financial gain, which I hope will allow me to retire early. But I do also love the hustle-bustle of day to day management of my properties."*

Let's not forget there are other places where you can spend your money. This book is not designed to tell you to invest in any asset class—all have their pros and cons. Instead, I'm assuming you are already a property owner/investor and simply want to know how to optimise the returns by self-managing and doing it the right way.

However, for completeness, let me add some examples of where else you could invest your money. I'm using very broad examples and groupings here for simplicity:

### 1.2.1 Other Places to Invest Your Money

- **Cash:** Cash is king, they say. And as a landlord, you should always make sure you keep some cash aside as a "rainy day" fund. It' s the safest way to store your money, which naturally means your return is low.

- **Stocks and shares:** Easy to invest in via the many apps and websites these days. My personal favourite is Hargreaves Lansdown. Pick individual stocks or sector/market trackers (i.e. FTSE 100 all share tracker). Easy to liquidate (get your money back out), but be aware that the value of your investment can go up or down, so make sure you understand what you are doing.

- **Other conventional investments:** You can stick money in currency markets (i.e. buy some Euros), you could buy commodities (i.e. buy some gold), or invest money in fixed income markets (i.e. government or company debt).

- **Less conventional investments:** There's ever new and exciting places you can store your money these days. It would not be possible to write any sort of book without mentioning cryptocurrency. Peer-to-peer lending is also big these days (ever heard of Funding Circle as the biggest example of this?). Or what about investing in start-ups? Check out Seedrs if you fancy that. Risks (and, in theory, returns) are higher for these types of investments. There are many more.

I'm not a qualified financial advisor (I'm just a lowly accountant), so please don't take my waffly points above as investment advice in any way. As long as you have an awareness of some ("some" being the keyword as many other investment opportunities exist) of the alternative areas outside of property, it means you'll be able to assess just how well your property is performing compared to those other areas.

Before you invest, speak to a qualified professional, or at the very least, make sure you understand what you are investing in.

Anyway, you decide where you want to keep your money.

This is a property book, so let me explain why I (and the other landlords I've asked) like a high proportion of my investments to be in property:

### 1.2.3 Advantages of Investing in Property

- **Ability to leverage:** Invest £50,000 in a bank account at 1% return and in one year's time, you will own £50,500.

Instead, if you invest £50,000 into a deposit to buy a £200,000 property, with a £150,000 interest-only mortgage where the value increases by 1% over the year and provides £3,000 annual profit (rental income less costs).

In one year's time, you'll have £3,000 in the bank and your equity will be £52,000 (£202,000 property value less £150,000 mortgage). Total profit of £5,000. That's a 10% return. Leverage is powerful. Imagine how big that gets if property prices go up by 5% or 10%? Or double over a number of years.

This is the key advantage you get from investing in property.

- **Inflation double whammy:** Over time, inflation pushes the value of your property higher (capital gain for you) and increases the rent you will receive. Even better if you have a mortgage, as this will shrink over time with inflation.

- **Low volatility:** The property market doesn't fluctuate each day like a stock market. It moves slowly, adjusting over time to longer-term market trends. That helps you sleep easier at night.

- **Strong returns vs risk:** Property pays so much more than putting cash in a bank account. Yes, there is more risk involved but so much less risk than some of the higher-earning investments.

- **Tangible:** Worry about your pension because you don't really know where it's invested? With property, you can touch it. And that makes people feel more comfortable. It's "safe as houses" as the phrase goes!

- **Cash flow:** Set your property up right and it provides an income. Cash (rent) sent to your bank account every month. For many landlords, this means they don't need a full-time job, or maybe it just means they don't need to rely so heavily on their employment income.

Property investment has always been a good investment. We all know that. But is that still the case?

## 1.3 The Challenges Landlords Now Face

Making money as a landlord was fairly easy 10-20 years ago. Minimal rules and the ability to borrow lots of money cheaply meant it was fairly easy to become a landlord. Money rolled in, property prices rose and landlords became wealthy.

Those golden days are gone. Sorry. But when you look more closely, I'd actually describe them as the cowboy years.

Easy money and minimal rules attract certain types. Tenants had very little protection and we all know what happened to the banks and lenders of these risky loans (hint: credit crunch, government bailout, global recession).

*"I rented a property at uni as a tenant, and when I moved out, the landlord just didn't return the deposit. Back then, there was no government registered deposit scheme and it took me almost a year of pursuing him through the legal system to get my money back."*

So, the property market has evolved since then, with a whole host of new property rules aimed at making the industry fairer and, more importantly, safer:

**Certificates:** You need a number of certificates to legally rent out a property—Energy Performance, Gas, HMO and Electrical Safety to name a few. All covered in detail later. These are great steps forward for the property industry in improving safety, but they come at a cost to landlords who are required to obtain and renew these every number of years.

**Deposits:** Must now be registered in a government-approved scheme. This is a necessity and a great thing for protecting both tenants and landlords, but it does cost landlords to register these, along with time spent on the admin work (learn how in a later chapter). Any disputes are settled independently, but it's widely known that favour is given to tenants. Whilst I agree this is the right approach from the independent adjudicator, costs can add up for landlords.

**Evictions:** So much harder. Again, good news for ensuring fairness and improving the property industry as a whole. The last thing you want is tenants not having legal rights to remain in properties, and at the mercy of scrupulous landlords wanting to boot them out. But for the bad apple tenants out there who don't pay rent or treat the property badly, unfortunate landlords now face an almighty battle to get them out of their property—at great effort and cost.

**Tax.** Of course, tax. If an industry or business are publicly seen to be making money, higher tax soon follows. Allowances have been removed, and new stricter (and in my opinion, unfair) taxes have been introduced.

For example, the 10% wear and tear allowances were removed, higher stamp duty charges are now levied and the dreaded S.24

restrictions to mortgage interest are now the bane of most landlords' lives. Long story short, landlords now pay more tax.

It's not just property rules that have made it harder for landlords. The world has and continues to change, which presents new challenges:

**Tenant expectations:** Are most definitely higher than they used to be. Social media and technology make it so much easier for tenants to shop around and they usually aren't afraid to request properties to be refurbished more to their liking as part of the rental negotiation. They want quicker and better service throughout the tenancy—expecting queries or repairs to be dealt with speedily. Certainly not unreasonable, but can be costly.

**Economy:** Then there's the macro market. It has not been so kind to us these last few years, has it? Credit crunch, Brexit uncertainty and the horror of COVID-19. Us landlords are business owners. And it's hard to run a stable and thriving business in such volatile and challenging external market conditions. Think lower rents, higher costs, more voids.

Just to throw a drop of positivity into the mix here, yes Brexit, COVID-19 and other factors have made the market more challenging. But just remember that there are still a lot of people coming in and out of the UK, and everyone needs somewhere to live. So, demand for property is always going to be high.

And finally (back to the negative, sorry!), have you noticed how expensive your high street agent fees are these days?

**Fees:** Have these crept up slowly over the years or just jumped right up? Probably both. There is a good reason for that, namely the introduction of the tenant fees ban. This stops landlords or agents being able to charge fees to tenants (i.e. for setting up the contract, general admin, deposit registration, obtaining references, preparing an inventory etc.).

And as a tenant myself, these fees were high. So, it's a good thing for tenants.

*"The previous place I lived in as a tenant a few years back, I was charged £150 for an inventory check-in report, and a further $150 for a tenancy agreement. Ouch!"*

However, fees charged to tenants used to be a useful source of income for high street agents. For example, they could set up a tenancy agreement and charge BOTH landlords and tenants for exactly the same contract. Same applies to most other charges. They can no longer do that.

But have high street agents suddenly had their income reduced by half? Nope. Their business model would be ruined overnight if that was the case. So, how do you think they supplement their lost income? Yes, YOU. Landlords wear that pain—more on that shortly.

Landlords have been hit from every angle. But looking back over those challenges, ask yourself: Which of these can I control, and thus mitigate?

You can't avoid the new rules as they are legal requirements, change tenant expectations or control what goes on with macro-economy. Tax to some extent can be optimised, but tax rules must still be followed.

But the one key area you can control is those higher agent fees that are eating away at your profit margins. In property, and life in general, it's important to focus on issues that are within your control. Make those areas better. Earn more money. That is what this book is about.

## 1.4 The High Street Agent, and Why They are Failing

Let's properly examine the business model of the high street agent.

I'd like to add a strong disclaimer here that this book is not a witch hunt against high street agents. Over the years, I've worked with 50+ agents. Yes, at times, I've been frustrated by their fees and level of service, but I've also worked with some really talented and professional individuals.

Unfortunately for them, the world has changed, and their traditional business model just doesn't work as well as it used to.

Even before COVID-19 changed the world as we know it, if you were to walk down any high street in the UK, you'd expect to see a few things: A Pret, a charity shop, a £1 store (actually, probably a few of these) and of course… a high street agent.

High street agents are part of our culture. As a nation, we are obsessed with property. Everyone will have dealt with high street agents in their lives as they help the people buy, sell or rent property. Let's face it, we all like browsing the adverts in their store windows.

And whilst COVID-19 has been particularly painful for high street agents, their business model has been in decline for quite some time. Here are three reasons why:

### 1) High street woes

Growing up, a trip to the high street was a real treat. shops, cafes, buzzing atmosphere. You name it, the high street provided it.

Anyone experienced that recently? Nope, didn' t think so.  And I'm talking pre-COVID-19 here. Every second shop is now boarded up. They resemble ghost towns, a place you quickly hurry through on your way home from work for fear of someone seeing you there. Oh, the embarrassment. Why shop on the high street when Amazon can deliver something right to your door, which is cheaper, better quality and in less time than it takes to make a cup of tea?

> *"Last year, 284 independent high street estate agents closed their doors, making it the sector with the highest number of closures followed by newsagents, women's clothing, fashion, delis and hairdressers."*

Well, spare a thought for high street agents, whose homes are well and truly stuck on the high street. Locked in to paying high rents to secure the most impressive spot on a deserted street. When it comes to business, we've all heard the phrase "Location, Location, Location". Well, for the high street agent, location was once their key selling point. It's now their nemesis.

## 2) Technology

Technology is great. We all use it. We all benefit from it. We are all probably negatively impacted by it (ever found yourself mindlessly scrolling through Facebook feeds?). And the property industry has certainly not escaped the technological evolution.

Let me focus on two key technological changes that are putting pressure on high street agents:

- **Online searching.** If you want to move house (buying or renting), do you a) wander up and down the high street in the rain trying to find a high street agent window to look in, or b) jump onto Rightmove, add your search criteria and find suitable properties in a matter of minutes? (HINT: Tick the second box.)

- **Online competition.** SPOILER ALERT. You can now buy, sell or rent property entirely online. There is no longer a need to use a high street agent! A whole host of online agents have popped up. These can provide all the services a traditional high street agent can offer (yes, even viewings) at a fraction of the price. You can even tailor your package to pick the exact services you want. Mind-blowing. This book will tell you all about how to use them.

**3) Lower revenue**

Imagine any business being told by the government that they are now no longer able to charge a significant chunk of their fees to customers. That's what the tenant fee ban did last year to estate agents.

> Under the Tenant Fees Act (2019), landlords or their agents are no longer allowed to charge tenants for anything except: the rent, the tenancy deposit and a holding deposit (more on these below).
>
> This means landlords or agents are no longer allowed to ask tenants to cover the cost of their own referencing, check-in, inventory reports, cleaning or admin fees.

How did high street agents react? Well, a large proportion of these lost tenant fees have been pushed to landlords as I mentioned earlier, but the reality is, they have also just had to accept reduced revenues. That's a bummer.

It's been a tough few years for high street agents. They have had to react to these new competitors and reduced revenues by reducing their cost base, which has had a knock-on impact on the level of service they offer to landlords. A vicious circle.

I don't like to focus on the negative, so I'll end this section on a more upbeat note. Yes, the business model of high street agents is facing more pressure than ever, and as a landlord, you are likely paying the price of that. But they will always have a place on the high street as there will always be buyers/sellers who need their help to facilitate property transactions.

## 1.5 What You Can Do About It

Back to the focus of this book...

So, the question is, are you happy with the service you are receiving from your high street agent and the fees you are paying? The fact you reading this book means your answer is likely "NO".

I'm willing to bet that you are what I call a "new era" landlord.

A "new era" landlord wants to increase their financial returns from property, improve the service they offer to tenants, understand the rules impacting the market they operate in, and utilise the new technology available.

To do that, you need to self-manage. It's time to "Ditch the High Street Agent".

## 1.6 Chapter Summary

- There is a huge array of financial and non-financial benefits of being a landlord.
- Owning a rental property offers many benefits over other forms of investment.
- Being a landlord has become significantly harder these last few years due to challenging market conditions and additional legal requirements.
- The business model of high street agents is struggling, with higher fees being charged to landlords as a result of this.
- For landlords wanting to increase their financial returns, provide a better service to tenants and be more involved, it's time to "Ditch the High Street Agent".

# 2.0 DECIDING IF SELF-MANAGING YOUR PROPERTY IS RIGHT FOR YOU

I want to teach you how you can save money and be a better landlord by self-managing your rental property.

But let's be sensible and make sure this change is right for you. It's not for everyone. We firstly need to weigh up the pros and cons, assess the numbers, and see how much time it will take so we can be sure this is the right change for YOU.

You can then make an informed and positive decision on the best way to manage your property.

Let's crunch those numbers…

*"I was scared initially about self-managing my property, but I'm now so glad I made that decision." (Rob Dighton, 2019)*

## 2.1 How Much Can YOU Save?

Let's face it, one of the main reasons that landlords move to self-managing is the substantial cost-savings they make. Which, in this challenging environment, matters more than ever. But there is no point talking about potential cost-savings or guesstimating what you think you might save.

Let's work out how much YOU can save. Right now.

To be clear, we are not going to calculate how much more your rental property makes you. Or consider costs that remain constant regardless of whether you self-manage. For the avoidance of doubt, let's list some of these:

- Mortgage expense
- Inventory check-in/out costs
- Costs of obtaining EPC, gas certificate, electrical certificate
- Costs to register deposits
- Costs to reference tenants

Instead, we are simply looking at the costs you pay using your current high street agent vs what you'd pay if you were self-managed. The difference is your saving. Something you'd make every year.

I'll use an actual example of one of my properties to guide you through the calculation.

**Step 1:** Calculate how much you are currently paying your high street agent, which likely includes costs such as:

a) Finders fee
b) Fully managed fee
c) Contract drafting/admin fee

*"I paid Hamptons 12% + VAT to fully manage my property. Monthly rent was £1,700, which equated to monthly fees of £245 (annual fees of £2,938). On top of that, I paid £280 for a contract. So, total fees of £3,218 a year. Every year."*

**Step 2:** Calculate how much you will pay to advertise when you self-manage.

You'll have to trust me here. I'll give you full details on expected costs in Chapter 3, but for now, I will give you an annual number you will likely pay. I'll use exact numbers that I've paid. £180. Yep, that's £180. You read it right. That includes:

a) Advertising fee

b) Registering tenant deposit

c) 2 x tenant references

d) Contracts preparation and e-signing

**Step 3:** Deduct high street agent costs from self-managing costs.

£3,218 high street agent fees - £180 self-manage fees =

wait for it… a difference of £3,038 (i.e. cost-saving).

**Step 4:** Tax. Assuming for simplicity you are a UK taxpayer, if your profit from your property changes, then there will be tax consequences, which will be based on the rate of tax you pay normally. For a basic rate taxpayer, that's a tax rate of 20%. Which means your true cost-saving from moving to self-managed is 80% of the number above:

£3,038 x 80% = £2,430.

**Step 5:** This is your annual number. Do you have more than one property? If so, you need to perform the same calculation for them.

Add them together. I have six properties, all now self-managed. That saving can quickly add up.

For me, I save approximately £2,430 x 6 = £14,580.

Every. single. year. Wow!

## 2.2 Is it Right for You?

By now, you should have a decent feel for how much money you can save by self-managing your property. And let's be fair, the money-saving is likely to be one of the biggest factors for most landlords in making the decision to switch.

Think about that money-saving in more detail first. Ask yourself how badly you want or need that saving each year. What could or would you spend it on instead? Does it represent a high proportion of your overall income? Do you have other sources of income? £2,500 of cost-saving a year is very important to some. To others, it may not make much difference to their overall income. Take a few minutes to consider how it would impact your life.

But money isn't—and should never be—the only factor in this decision. Let's think about your own time…

### 2.2.1 How Much Time Does it Take to Self-Manage?

Let's start with the obvious: It will take up more of your time if you self-manage your rental property rather than having a high street agent do this for you.

The key question is, how much more time? Unfortunately, there is no simple or consistent answer to that.

There are so many variables that influence how much time it will take. For example, if you let your property on the first tenant viewing, that won't take up much time. However, that doesn't always happen, sadly!

Likewise, if no repairs are required on your property, you probably won't hear from your tenants and won't spend any time on property management. Conversely, multiple maintenance issues will take up much more of your time.

Let me try to break the "time cost" down into the different stages of self-management with some examples of the time spent so you can get a rough feel for what it would involve for you.

Important to note here is that I'm not going to cover items that take the same time for self-managing as they do when using a high street agent, including:

- **Rental contracts:** I'll show you how your new online agent will prepare these for you (for free!).

- **References:** A professional referencing agency will perform these for you when you self-manage. No extra work needed.

- **Deposit registration:** Your online agent will do this for you. All you need to do is sign.

- **Landlord insurance:** You'll need to arrange this yourself regardless of whether you self-manage.

- **Rent collection:** Your online agent will usually facilitate this for you. Just check your bank account once a month to ensure it's received.

- **Inventory reports:** In most cases, your online agent will sort this for you. I occasionally organise myself, but the time spent is so little, it's not worth going into detail.

- **Legal documents:** I'll cover all you need to know on the legal documents, but long story short, as long as you know about what's needed, someone else will sort the necessary certificates for you.

So, where exactly will all this extra time be spent? Let's assume that you advertise and let your property for a full year, after which your tenant will leave and you will need to find a new one (in reality, I'd hope tenants would often stay longer so time spent would be lower, but let's look at worst-case scenarios to give a fair picture):

- **Constructing the advert:** You will need to register with an online agent (easy), and then add details for your property to their portal so it can be advertised online. It's a one-time cost, which, using the hints I give you later, won't take any more than a few hours. Future advertising is a two-minute copy/paste job.

  *ADVERT TIME: Two hours.*

- **Managing tenant enquiries and viewings:** This is the big one.

Initially, you'll spend an hour or two (broken out into lots of small time chunks) liaising with tenants on when they can view the property.

Viewings themselves take up the most time. If you are efficient, you can get multiple viewings done in the same day in a few hours' time, after which you get an offer that you accept. It can take multiple days of viewings though.

Here's where proximity to the property matters. If you live four hours away and attend multiple viewings, the time spent will jump up very quickly. Let's assume you are an hour away and it takes two days of viewings to secure an acceptable offer (note that the negotiation part is the same if you self-manage or use a high street agent):

*MANAGING TENANT ENQUIRIES: Two hours*

*VIEWINGS TIME: Five hours*

*TRAVEL TIME: Four hours*

- **Check-in/check-out:** At both check-in and check-out, you will need to visit the property to hand over or collect the keys from the tenants. You will use this visit to assess the property condition and give tenants an overview of how the property works (saves you many hours later!).

*CHECK-IN/OUT TIME: Six hours (Inc. travel)*

- **Property visits:** Let's assume you visit the property once a year outside of check-in/check-out:

*PROPERTY VISIT TIME: Two and a half hours (Inc. travel)*

- **Maintenance issues:** Based on my self-management of my properties (which I've automated as much as possible), I'd estimate this to be three hours a year. My time spent is purely admin time—I don't clean or fix things myself, instead, I always get tradespeople or cleaners to sort these items. I'd recommend you do the same, unless you are proficient in this area or enjoy it.

*PROPERTY MAINTENANCE TIME: Two and a half hours*

- General admin: There's bound to be a few other admin items that pop up when you self-manage, so let's throw in some buffer for this.

*ADMIN TIME: One hour*

So, how much is that?

I make that 25 hours a year in total, per property.

*"If I'm totally honest, I spend a lot less time self-managing my properties than 25 hours per year. My tenants stay on average longer than one year (so much less check-in/out time). I've never not let my property in the first day of viewings and I have tradespeople that undertake proper visits on my behalf."*

But I want you to see a higher "time spent" number. Much better to make your decision to switch to self-managed based on a time estimate of 25 hours per year, then be pleasantly surprised if it takes up less time than initially thought.

> Pro landlord tip: Think about how the 25 hours of extra time spent compares to the (in my example) cost-saving of £2,430 per year. My hourly rate is £2,430 annual saving / 25 hours = £97.2 per hour. Time well spent for me. What is the same number for you?

How does 25 hours a year sound? Works out to be roughly two hours a month, or 30 minutes a week (on average, of course!). Can you spare that time? Surely you can!

We'll come onto the concept of "myths" shortly, but as a clue (spoiler alert!), worrying about not having enough time to self-manage their property is a common landlord fear before making the switch.

As you'll find out in this book, we'll consider each of these worries, unknowns and doubts (the myths) and bust them up!

Myth: "I won't have the time to self-manage my rental property."

BUSTED!

Time constraints are such a common doubt of landlords reluctant to make the switch to self-managing. You probably already have a full-time job. Surely you can't start doing another one?

Well, luckily, you don't have to! It only takes 25 hours a year, on average to self-manage your rental property. That's not much at all.

This book will teach you how to systemise each of the parts of self-management for maximum efficiency, to ensure it takes up as little of your time as possible.

And I should know… I balance a busy job, two young kids and self-manage six rental properties. Trust me, it's do-able, as long as you do it right!

As well as the cost-savings, and the additional time constraints, there are many other important factors to think about before you make your decision.

I've added a list of the positive and negative considerations of self-managing your rental property below. Their relevance will depend on

YOUR circumstances, so read through the list and consider which ones are important to you:

Note: Some are listed as both pros and cons!

### 2.2.2 Advantages of Self-Managing

- **More control over your property:** You make all the decisions. It's your asset, after all.

- **See first-hand the condition of your property:** No need to rely on agent feedback or inventory reports. Seeing how things look yourself can enable you to make better decisions.

*"For years, I relied on agents' feedback and inventory reports, and believed my flat was in decent condition. When I visited it for the first time in many years after switching to self-managed, I saw first-hand just how much work was needed to attract the right tenants. An email or piece of paper just doesn't capture reality." (James, landlord)*

- **Choose tenants yourself:** They say gut instinct is a powerful tool, and self-managing your rental property allows you to use this tool. This, combined with professional referencing reports, puts you in a perfect position to select great tenants.

- **Better advertising of your property:** Only you can "sell" (and by "sell" I mean market/advertise) the property best and most accurately when advertising it. It's your highest priority as getting good tenants in fast means more cash in your pocket, so you are more incentivised than anyone to get this done well.

- **Offer tenants faster, better service.** No more middleman high street agent delays. You can think of them as customers and treat them as such, offering great service that increases the chances of tenants staying for many years.

*"My old agent contacted me to say there was an issue with the heating at my property that they would have fixed. Two months later, the tenants reached out directly to say the heating still wasn't working. This just doesn't happen now I self-manage the property!" (Carly, landlord)*

- **Reduce risk:** A property is an expensive asset, arguably not something you'd want to leave in the hands of someone who doesn't care as much as you. Why trust (hope/risk) someone else to ensure your compliance with the many rules and regulations? Want a job done right, do it yourself.

- **More personal relationship:** Tenants get to meet and liaise with a real person (YOU), someone who they know cares. You get direct feedback on the property from your tenants. Read any media source and you wouldn't believe this, but you can build a trusting and friendly relationship with tenants.

*"Since the move to self-managing, my relationship with my tenants has gone from strength to strength. I treat them like valued customers, and in turn, have had respectful and caring tenants. Win-win for all." (Rupert, Bournemouth landlord)*

- **Utilise and develop your skillset:** The right type of landlord is someone who likes being involved, has good people skills, is organised, inquisitive and prepared to take some risks. You get to put these skills into practice and develop them as you go.

- **Have fun!** At the end of the day, you need to like—or at least partially like—property. If that's you, you can have a lot of fun self-managing your rental property. It gives you a sense of purpose. Live it. Love it.

There are many, many advantages to self-managing. Not just the substantial cost-savings!

However, I want this book to give a balanced view on self-managing your rental property. So, let's not shy away from some of the inevitable disadvantages associated with self-managing.

### 2.2.3 Disadvantages of Self-Managing

- **Can be more stressful:** Implementing the systems and mindset that I cover in this book will help minimise stress, but inevitably, there will be some additional stress when you deal with the day to day management yourself.

- **On call 24/7:** In theory, anyway. In reality, this doesn't happen that much. In 10+ years of being a landlord, I've never been called at midnight, on Sunday, or on Christmas Day (fortunately). But it can happen, so bear it in mind.

- **A more personal relationship:** Having this direct, more personal relationship with tenants and tradespeople can be great. But it does also mean you have to deal with any potential awkward conversations yourself (think rent negotiations or deposit deductions). Are you equipped to deal with these without undue stress? Not everyone likes it.

- **Proximity to the property itself:** Do you live close(ish) to your property such that you can travel there without too much inconvenience? That's needed if you want to be a self-managing landlord. "Inconvenience" is obviously subjective, but I'd quantify it as within one to two hours away. If you live overseas or much further away than that, it can make it much harder to self-manage, albeit not impossible.

*"All of my properties are within one and a half hours from where I live, which works out fine for me. I don't travel to them frequently, but can do so fairly easily if I ever need to."*

### 2.2.4 Decision Time

There' s lots to think about! You now know how much extra money you'll have in your pocket each year, and some of the other considerations like how much extra time it will take up. Don't overthink it. Remember, this is not a once-in-a-lifetime decision. You can always switch back, or make the decision to change in a year from now.

What does your gut tell you?

My final point in aiding your decision is a simple question: Do you like property? Is it something you find interesting, that you want to be actively involved in? If yes, it's most definitely time to switch to being a self-managed landlord!

If it's not for you, that's fine. You've assessed your options now at least. And the content in this book is still useful as it teaches you what you need to know as a landlord, so read on regardless.

It's only right that I remind you of that BIG FAT DISCLAIMER at the front of this book. I have switched to being a self-managing landlord, and find myself wealthier, more knowledgeable, happier and with better tenants. However, only you can decide whether this switch is right for you based on your own circumstances. You already knew that though, didn't you?

## 2.3 The Myths

Let's assume that you've calculated the financial impact of switching to being a self-managing landlord and you like the sound of the extra cash. You've got an idea of how much time it will take, and worked through the other advantages and disadvantages of switching and can easily see what will be best for you. I'd imagine most landlords these days would reach the same conclusion you've just reached—to switch.

Yet so many landlords don't switch. "Why on earth would they not switch?!" I hear you scream in bewilderment.

It's because of the myths. Sounds spooky, right?

Well, that's because the myths are scary. They are at first, anyway, until you know better. As I made my first switch from using high street agents to self-managing my properties, there were so many things I was **worried** about, it felt like there were so many things I didn't know (**unknowns**) and I had so many **doubts** on whether I had the ability to perform the same duties as a high street agent.

> The "myths" are the common worries, unknowns and doubts that are experienced by landlords when they switch from using a high street agent to self-managing their rental property

From talking to other landlords who have made the same switch to self-managing their rental property, it turns out these worries, unknowns and doubts are commonplace. It's a normal human emotion when faced with change.

Let's have a look at these common myths—there are 13 of them obviously:

## ***<u>THE MYTHS</u>***

*<u>Worries</u>*

*"I'm worried I'll choose a bad tenant who will trash my property or won't pay me rent."*
*"I'm worried about complying with all the legal requirements."*
*"I'm worried my tenant will call me at midnight on Sunday every week."*
*"I'm worried I won't be able to get tenants out of my property if I need to."*

*<u>Unknowns</u>*

*"I don't know how to advertise my property to find tenants."*
*"I don't know how much rent to charge."*
*"I don't know how to draft a tenancy agreement."*
*"I don't know how to collect and register a tenants' deposit."*
*"I don't know how to find and/or work with good tradespeople."*

*<u>Ability doubts</u>*

*"I can't deal with the stress of day to day management of my property."*
*"I'm not organised enough to deal with all the admin of self-managing my property."*
*"I won't have the time to self-manage my rental property."*
*"I won't have anyone to ask for help if I need it."*

Can you relate to any/all of these? I bet you can.

The whole reason for me writing this book is not just to tell you how to make the switch to being a self-managing landlord. When you go about the switch, I want you to feel confident on each step of the journey. I don't want you to experience these worries, unknowns and doubts. Especially because you don't have to. Because they are just myths. Ghosts, really (you see what I'm building up to here, don't you?).

On the switching to self-managing landlord journey, I've been there, done that, and felt every emotion under the sun.

Which puts me in the perfect position to share these myths, and importantly why they are unfounded. How, with the right knowledge and mindset (that you will learn in this book), you can easily mitigate these myths.

The myth busters as I've excitedly called them. Throughout the book, I'll identity the myths in each of the relevant sections, then explain how the myth busters allow you to zap those worries, unknowns and doubts, and confidently work through the steps required to self-manage your rental properties.

Bustin' makes me feel good.

## 2.4 Taking the Plunge – What Happens Next?

Newsflash. Once you've made the decision to switch to self-managing, the change itself doesn't happen overnight.

That's because YOU should choose when it's best for you to implement this change.

If the property is vacant, then now is probably a good time to start self-managing.

Another good time to move to self-managing is if existing tenants have given in their notice. This gives a clear and easy cut-off for you to take over the running of the property.

However, if the property has existing tenants (regardless of whether their term is near to ending or not), there are some steps to follow to ensure a smooth transition.

### 2.4.1 Liaise with Your High Street Agent

Firstly, review the contract with your current high street agent (this is not the tenancy agreement you will have in place with your tenant). This should stipulate a notice period, typically three to six months.

Give written notice to your high street agent of your decision that you no longer require their service. I' ve found the best way is to then follow this up with a polite call.

Make sure you provide good and honest feedback to them, along with your reasons for switching to self-managing, as this will help their business learn and improve.

### 2.4.2: Inform Your Tenants

What type of landlord do you want to be? Hopefully, one who treats a tenant like a customer, someone who aims to provide them not with just a service, but a home where they can feel comfortable and happy. Therefore, this first direct contact with your tenant is really important. You are setting the scene for your future relationship together.

Here's how to get it right:

✓ This may be your first direct contact with your tenants, so be sure to give a proper introduction and warm welcome when you reach out. First impressions count!

✓ You can contact them by letter, email or message. You can even call, although I'd always suggest doing this only as a follow-up to avoid taking them by surprise. I'd also suggest choosing what medium of communication you intend to use with them going forward to set expectations correctly from the outset.

✓ Be sure to mention when the high street agent' s management of the property ends and yours begins, as well as your contact details.

✓ Reassure them that this does not impact their tenancy agreement contract between the landlord (YOU) and the tenant (them). It's important to mention this to avoid causing any alarm.

✓ Provide your contact details as well as any other useful numbers (handymen, etc.).

✓ Inform them that their deposit continues to be protected in a registered government scheme. No impact to them here.

✓ Reassure tenants. This move will allow them to receive better service (quicker, more personal).

✓ Let them know that the only change is that payment of rent should be made directly to you. Give clear instructions of when the standing order should be transferred.

### 2.4.3: Agent Handover

It's important to discuss the tasks the high street agent will continue to be responsible for during the final few weeks/months of your contract with them.

There is a risk here that the tenant may be neglected if the high street agent is not focusing on their needs, and you have not yet started the management.

*"Whilst my agents had three months' notice, I generally started self-management as soon as I'd given notice to ensure the tenant received good care and we started our new relationship on a positive footing."*

It's also crucial to clarify who has the tenant's deposit and will be responsible for that going forward.

If the high street agent holds the funds and has protected this in one of the government-approved schemes, that' s fine. A written notification from them that they will continue to hold this until the eventual end of the tenants' contract is fine.

If, like me, you would prefer funds in your own account for safe-keeping, you can request the high street agent to transfer the deposit to your bank account. There is no need to re-register the deposit with the government scheme. Be clear and upfront with the tenant and ensure that the tenants' deposit is protected in a scheme AT ALL TIMES.

Don't forget keys. The high street agent will likely have at least one spare set of keys to the property. Depending on when you will take over the management of the property, you will need to arrange these being returned to you.

Some high street agents will have helped or handled the utilities for your property. They may need to help with the changeover of contact details with utility companies.

And finally, most high street agents will hold a float, whereby they keep a small sum, often £100-£500 of your money to cover maintenance items, etc. That's your money, so don't forget to ask for it back, and be sure to check each of your final few statements to ensure they are correct.

Once all done, don't forget to send a note to the high street agent thanking for them for all their work over the years. Professional, polite, business-orientated landlord. That is YOU now.

And that's it. Congratulations. You are now officially a self-managing landlord. You are about to make more money, and provide tenants with a better level of service. Give yourself a pat on the back.

## 2.6 Chapter Summary

- It's important to calculate how much you can save by switching to being a self-managing landlord—it's usually a lot!
- There are many different advantages and disadvantages of self-managing your rental property you need to consider before deciding to switch.
- The "myths" are the common worries, unknowns and doubts that landlords experience that often stop them making the switch—and they are all unfounded. Busted!
- If you decide to switch, you need to follow certain practical steps to correctly deal with your tenant and high street agent.

# 3.0 ADVERTISING YOUR PROPERTY

One of the main reasons landlords are nervous about switching to self-managing their rental property is that they don't believe they can advertise their property as well as an established high street agent. Wrong!

Like most things in life, advertising can be done 100% online now. It's very easy and doesn't take up much of your time. Follow the simple steps in this chapter to find out how.

You'll also learn how to construct the perfect advert, how much rent to charge and loads of pro-landlord tips for making your rental property truly stand out from the competition.

*"90% of tenants now conduct all their property searches online. No one walks along a high street hoping to find a place to live."*

## 3.1 How to Advertise Your Property Online

Over 90% of all rental properties are now found on the major search portals. I'm sure you've heard of them: Rightmove, Zoopla, etc. If not, give it a go. Go onto *www.Rightmove.com* and within minutes, you can search for any type of property, anywhere. Other search portals exist but these main two are where the action is at.

Now let's set the record straight, you can't log in to Rightmove and directly list your property. Only registered agents can do that.

But don't fret. There is a very easy solution. Welcome to the world of the online agent.

### 3.1.1 What is an Online Agent?

The online agent is a relatively new concept in the landlord/lettings scene and is growing at exponential speed. A new one seems to pop up every week. They usually offer most of the same services as a traditional high street agent, but as the name suggests, they operate with an online presence only.

With no expensive premises to pay for, it means they are significantly cheaper than a high street agent. And guess who benefits from those lower costs? YOU do!

These online agents are able to offer the same services that high street agents offer. Confused given they supposedly are online only? Are these online agents magic?

Let me explain: They do have a physical office, but that can be anywhere in the country. They then have a network of nationwide coverage of the relevant people they need, including inventory clerks, handymen, and even people who conduct viewings at their/your request. The same as a high street agent really, except they don't work around the corner from your property.

Not only are they MUCH cheaper than a high street agent, they are also much more flexible in terms of allowing landlords to opt only for services you want—rather than being forced into a package deal. With online agents, you can do whatever you want, as customers should be able to do.

*"I only wanted an agent to list my rental property on the portals and then sort the tenancy agreement once I'd found tenants. Nothing else. My online agent made this so easy." (Pru, Croydon landlord)*

To me, the key benefit of online agents is that you can advertise a property on the major search portals (i.e. Rightmove) for as little as £29. Yes, that's just £29!

You then simply add what extra services you need. Want someone to arrange an EPC for you? Order that from the online agent and they'll book it in for you at a small cost. Want them to issue standard tenancy agreements and protect your tenants' deposit? Easy stuff for them. You name it, they can do it.

Want to take it a step further and pay for them to conduct viewings, or even provide a fully managed service? Guess what, they can also do that, and it still works out significantly cheaper than using a high street agent.

My personal opinion is that it's best not to take the fully managed service that online agents offer or have them conduct tenant viewings—here's why:

- **Local knowledge:** Online agents are not physically situated near your property, so don't have close interaction with local handymen, plumbers or other tradespeople. I think you, as a landlord (assuming you are local), can do this much better and build a long-term relationship with the key people who will maintain your house over the years. Do this part yourself.

- **Viewings:** One of the key advantages of moving to online agents (aside from the obvious extra dosh in your pocket) is that you, the person who cares most about your rental property, gets to meet and personally vet new tenants. You can also build a prosperous and mutually beneficial long-term relationship with them. Personally, I wouldn't want to hand over such an important part of my landlord duties to someone else, even if it is cheap and time effective with online agents.

This is just my personal take on how best to use online agents. Everyone is different though and that's the beauty of their model. They allow landlords to have complete control and flexibility over what you do yourself vs what you pay someone else to do. Perfect.

### 3.1.2 So, Who Are These "Online Agents" ?

The answer is...

There are many. And new ones are springing up all the time. Let me list out those I've worked with, as well as ones I'm aware of and heard good reviews about. In order to stay sane, I'll limit this to just a handful of online agents (apologies to those I'm not covering), but if you google "online letting agent", you'll find many more.

For each of these, I'll give a lightning quick overview, and if that tickles your fancy, just hop onto their website to get the latest details on the packages they offer (which change frequently). I'll start with my favourite:

Makeurmove
*https://www.makeurmove.co.uk/*

I love Makeurmove. I've used them for a good number of years now and have let numerous properties with them.

I use their basic "Good Landlord" package, which, for £15 a month allows me to list my property on the major portals, hep facilitate tenant viewings, prepare electronic contracts, perform 2x referencing, and even rent collection. An absolute bargain.

What I love most about Makeurmove is how they combine efficient automated flows throughout the letting process, but also have a personal feel to them—you can pick up the phone and speak to someone quickly and easily. Great service, at a reasonable price··· what's not to love?!

Openrent

*https://www.openrent.co.uk/*

Openrent are the big dogs when it comes to online letting. The biggest property lettings agent in the UK!

They offer a ridiculously cheap £29 to advertise your property on the major portals, and only charge £49 if you want them to sort the contracts and deposit registration.

Their online system is fully automated to take you through the process. I use Openrent, along with many landlords, and I've not heard a bad word about them yet.

You can use the link below to get a free trial:

*openrent.co.uk/invite/2259012*

Howsy

*https://howsy.com/*

These guys are going places. Quick expansion driven by offering great service driven by modern technology.

Their renter find package starts at £149 a year, and you can add on extra services right up to fully managed services. Worth a look.

Mashroom

*https://mashroom.com/*

I've not used Mashroom but have heard great reviews about them on many online landlord forums. Offering a 30-day free listing on the major search portals as the starting point, you can then bolt on what additional services you need. Services for landlords, by landlords.

99 home

*https://www.99home.co.uk/*

They offer sales, letting and wider property services. The most common package is the £29 express package, and you've guessed it... you can add extra services as suits your needs.

Lettingaproperty

*https://www.lettingaproperty.com/*

This is another one I've heard good reviews about in landlord online forums. They offer many different packages, and what I particularly like is how they set out their package comparison page so you can see exactly what you do/don't get for each package, making your decision much easier.

Iamtheagent

*https://www.iamtheagent.com/*

20% discount to NHS workers. Nice touch, along with comparisons of how much you can save vs using a high street agent. The usual range of packages are offered, with (dare I say it) the trendiest website of the lot!

So many to choose from…

### 3.1.3 Which One for You?

My main tip—as it often is in life—is not to overthink it. Yes, there are some differences, but with all of these, you will save a lot of money over using a high street agent, and also be given a great deal more flexibility over the services you purchase.

*"I spent hours comparing each of the packages offered by online agents when I first switched. In reality, all the online agents I've used have offered a good service at a great price—just pick one!"*

If I was forced to choose, I'd have Makeurmove as my personal favourite. To me, they offered fantastic value for money but with a personal feel and efficient service. I really felt valued as a customer whenever I picked up the phone to speak to them.

### 3.1.4 What Next?

I'll use Makeurmove as an example to guide you through the next steps. In reality, they all work in a similar way so these steps will work for you whichever online agent you end up going with.

Firstly, register and purchase the package that works best for you. Again, don't overthink it as you can always bolt on extras at a later date.

Personally, I'd recommend the standard "Good Landlord" advertising package on Makeurmove, costing £180, paid in instalments over 12 months.

For this, Makeurmove will list your property advert on major portals, help coordinate tent viewings via their online platform, issue electronic tenancy agreements, reference two tenants and even collect rent on your behalf. Awesome value for money!

Once purchased, it's time to add the details of your property. Work through their simple steps, including how many rooms your property has, where it's located, etc. All very simple stuff.

## 3.2 Constructing the Advert

This is such an important part of renting property, and now you are a self-managing landlord, YOU will be in charge of this. Which is perfect because the job itself is not difficult if you follow the tips in this chapter. As YOU care the most for your property, you are the most motivated to getting this right.

It's important to think about how a tenant searches for properties. We can then ensure the advert is best placed to grab their attention. Tenants firstly enter their basic search criteria, let's assume in Rightmove:

1) Area (i.e. within 1km of Clapham Junction)
2) Property type (1-2 bedroom flats)
3) Price range (£1,250-£1,500 per month)

The property portals will display the results. Usually, lots of them! 99 times out of 100 tenants will skim through the numerous options, looking first at photos, and then description. Lots stop at photos, sometimes even the first photo. If still interested, they might then look at other features, floorplans, etc.

So, let's go through your advert in that order to make sure you get it right (obviously, you can't do much about the location or type—a one bed flat Clapham can't be sold as a two-bedroom flat in Chelsea!). Let's start with photos.

### 3.2.1 The Photos

GOOD PHOTOS ARE KEY. I can't emphasise this enough. Think of job interviews, or a first date. First impressions (first 10 seconds it is said) really count. This is how long tenants will take to make their first impression on your property.

A set of clear, nicely presented and well-lit photos will sell your property quickly. They make it stand out from the competition. Bad photos will turn customers off immediately, and within seconds, they will be looking at the next Rightmove property, never to return to yours again. Do not fail in this area.

*"I tried to save myself some money when I first started out by doing my own photos on my phone. Big mistake. When I look back, they were terrible!" (Bruno, Worcester landlord)*

As with most things in property, this is common sense and not difficult. Unless you are a professional photographer with a snazzy camera bigger than your own leg, do not do this yourself. Please.

Pay an actual property photography professional to do it the right way. It is not expensive. Makeurmove charge £99 for a set of professional photos. Order within a few minutes online and they will organise a photographer to attend your property. Let the pro do their work. You keep the files so can use them again and again for future adverts, so this is a one-off cost.

If you do decide to do it yourself (please don't!), then at least take these simple tips:

- Try to have no tenants present to avoid clutter
- Turn lights on
- Add items to make rooms look nicer (lay a table, add a plant in a room, bottle of wine on a balcony table, etc.) to sell the property as best as you can. You want prospective tenants to feel they want to live there. Sell the lifestyle they will have in your property.
- If the property has certain key features (large bathroom, new kitchen, large garden, etc.), include multiple shots of this to draw attention to it.

Think online dating photos. Best bits on show!

What else to include? Well, the inside of the property itself is not the only thing tenants are considering. What about the local park or shops, the block/street it is on, the view from a balcony, an area of interest nearby. Include photos of these. You are selling a lifestyle here. The tenant will live and breathe this area, so let them know what benefits await.

Take yourself or order online, and then upload your photos to your profile. You can even add a small caption to the photo if you feel it's needed.

### 3.2.2 The Description

Ok, you are a tenant looking for a property to rent. You've entered your search criteria, flicked through some photos of those on the search list at the top and found one with great photos. What do you do next?

You click on the description to find out more. So, as a landlord, at no extra cost, you are given an opportunity to sell your property more. Don't miss this opportunity. Write something that stands out and differentiates from the competition.

Let's be clear here. There is no right or wrong way of doing this. You don't need to be a professional writer or "qualified" high street agent. You just need to know your own property, and know what its strengths or special points are.

Put yourself in the tenants' shoes. What would they like to know? Here are some ideas:

- A high level overview.
- What type of tenant it would suit.
- Describe the rooms, mentioning any standout features (new kitchen, large double bedroom, great view, well-lit, etc.).
- Add details of what furniture is provided/offered and whether you are flexible on this.
- When is the property available?
- List advantages of the block or street (nice neighbours, quiet area, etc.).
- What local attractions are nearby that would appeal to your target tenants (schools, business parks, gyms, tourist attractions, shops, restaurants, parks, etc.)?
- Transport links (trains, buses, key roads).
- Other amenities (car parking, concierge, etc.).

- Extras (direct let with landlord, will be professionally cleaned prior to move-in date, preferred/flexible tenancy durations, deposit arrangements).

What words can you use? Whatever you want. Need some help? Go on Rightmove and search for properties, then read a few profiles and write down any words that stand out and sell their properties well. See if you can build these in. And remember, it doesn't have to be perfect, so don't overthink it!

Here's some examples of powerful property advert words that I love to use—there are many more!

- Stunning
- Spacious
- Cosy
- Must see
- Sought after
- Modern
- Stylish

And here's an example description of one of my properties. Feel free to copy and paste it, then update it with your own property details to save time:

MUST SEE 2 BEDROOM APARTMENT IN CENTRAL GREENWICH!

We are delighted to offer this stunning two-bedroom, two-bathroom apartment, situated within the popular ABC development in a highly desirable area of Greenwich.

The apartment is on the top floor and has a large wrap around balcony with stunning uninterrupted and panoramic views of Canary Wharf and The City.

The apartment comes unfurnished and is finished to a high standard, with wooden floors and modern appliances throughout. The main bedroom is large and has an en-suite. The second bedroom is well suited to be an office, second bedroom or nursery room, making this apartment perfect for a professional couple or small family.

The development itself is modern and includes a number of on-site features:

- Concierge
- Gymnasium/Crèche (fees apply)
- Numerous Shops/Restaurants

Living here, you will be able to easily enjoy the community feel within the development, as well as the world-famous delights of Greenwich, with the beautiful park, River Thames, Cutty Sark, Royal Observatory, Old Naval College and market, along with the high street shops and restaurants, all within a short walk from the apartment.

The apartment is located right next to Greenwich mainline and DLR station, offering fantastic transport connections, including:

- London Bridge – 8 mins by train
- Canary Wharf – 9 mins by DLR
- Bank – 19 mins by DLR
- Numerous local bus connections
- Less than an hour to Gatwick & London City airports
- 25 mins drive to M25 Motorway
- Thames Clipper boat connections to central London/The O2
- Note: This property does NOT come with parking

Viewings are highly recommended. The property is let directly by the landlord who, once you register your interest, will contact you to answer any of your initial questions over the phone before setting up a viewing slot.

Pretty good, right? I took words from other adverts I'd seen which impressed me, and combined it with my practical knowledge of the flat/area to create what I'd modestly describe as an awesome advert!

There is one other thing you must do. You need to list roughly 10 key highlights from your property, which are added at the top of the advert. You can take these from the description you've already written, so they could be "top floor apartment" or "well presented" or "excellent transport connections". Pick whichever points you feel best sell your flat. Don't overthink this, just go with your gut. Five minutes of work, no more.

Add a similar description and highlights to your online profile.

### 3.2.3 Floorplan

Most tenants will have already made their decision on whether they like your property just by looking at your photos and reading your description. But not all. Some prospective tenants want to visualise the property before they view it.

*"I used to get so many questions on my flat size from prospective tenants that I now add a floorplan to the advert to pre-empt these questions." (Sarah, landlord)*

A floorplan is needed here and is an excellent addition to your advert. Super easy to book via your online agent at a low cost (and once done, the floorplan is yours forever at no extra costs for future marketing).

If you don't have one, it's worth ordering online, then uploading a floorplan.

### 3.2.4 Video

Although not common, you can also purchase a video walk-around of your property. Yes, there is more upfront cost involved, but in the long run, this can save you a lot of cost as it can be sent to tenants before they view. This will give you a much better conversion rate of those who do view it, and save you time on wasted viewings.

Again, you only need to purchase this once and it really helps differentiate a property. Also, COVID-19 friendly!

I don't think this is essential, which means you could just do this yourself so you have it to hand in case a tenant requests it on an ad hoc basis.

Anyway, you now know all the different practical aspects on how to advertise your property to find tenants. Which means it's time to bust a myth…

Myth: "I don't know how to advertise my property to find tenants!"

BUSTED!

Advertising is one of the main barriers stopping landlords from self-managing their properties. New landlords just don't know where or how to do this. That is no longer the case for you.

You know that in a few simple clicks (from your sofa if you want), you can advertise your property online extremely cheaply and easily. Time to bag yourself a tenant.

Which nicely brings us on to one of the big questions landlords always ask....

## 3.3 How Much Rent to Charge

The eternal and impossible to answer question faced by every landlord. Each situation is different and depends on factors like the macro-economic environment, competition in general, and at the time you are advertising, the season and just good old-fashioned luck—maybe a tenant has just moved to the area and is desperate to find a place to live and is willing to pay over the odds to secure your property. Just maybe!

Let me give you a few practical tips on how to choose an appropriate level of rent to advertise your property, and also a few examples of the common pitfalls that landlords often succumb to (myself included!), as well as how much money you can save by knowing this.

### 3.1.1 Tip 1: Ask Your Current Tenant

If you have a reasonable relationship with your current tenant, what harm is there in asking for their opinion? After all, they have been living there and will know from a tenant' s perspective whether the amount they are paying represents good value or not. They have likely talked to their neighbours and will have sourced the competition in the area with a tenant's perspective rather than a biased landlord perspective.

*"I got on great with my previous Colindale tenants. They told me they had put in an offer of £150 lower than advertised rent (which, I'd accepted) just to try their luck, even though they were willing to pay full asking price."*

Does the above story make me feel like I've undervalued the property? Not at all. The tenants stayed for three and a half years and looked after the place like it was their own. They loved living there and dealt with maintenance, which meant I had no renewal costs, maintenance costs or void periods. That's worth its weight in gold.

### 3.3.2 Tip 2: Rightmove It

Go on Rightmove or Zoopla, enter a search criteria which will capture the wider area your property resides, and the property type (i.e. three-bedroom house) and look at the results.

How many are listed? Hundreds or just a few? A large amount of similar properties *could* indicate a tough market to list your property. Conversely, hardly any properties *could* be a sign of a poor rental market. *Could* being the keyword, remember these are just indicators. I firmly believe every property will let, just at the right price.

What is the lowest price offered? And highest? And average? How much are the comparable properties, i.e. similar area or specification offered for?

*"Consider listing your property at just under a round number, i.e. rather than £1,800 per month, go for £1,799 to catch all those tenants who search for LESS than £1,800 per month!"*

Final point on Rightmove pricing, remember you can advertise a property with a weekly rent, or a monthly rent. I always use monthly, as I feel weekly is a bit old-fashioned. But if you need to, just convert monthly into weekly by:

Monthly price x 12 / 52 weeks = weekly price

And then obviously weekly price x 52 / 12 monthly price.

Just stick to monthly though!

### 3.3.3 Tip 3: The Dreaded Void - How Much Would it Cost You?

Speaking to tenants or searching on Rightmove will have given you an initial feel for how much you could list your property at. I'm pretty sure the value you are leaning towards will be too high—human bias makes it almost impossible for landlords not to push for a slightly higher price than "true" market value.

But consider this: A higher listed price can (certainly not always) mean a longer void period—a period where NO rental income is received. Why? Because it will take you longer to find tenants. And that time costs money.

You need to know how much that void costs. Knowing this is crucial—you will make better decisions as a result. There's two things you need to calculate. For both, let me use the actual numbers from a property of mine that was un-let (void) at the initial time of writing… it went a few weeks later!

### 3.3.3.1 Calculate Actual Cash Outflow During the Void

This is easy to work out. Since the day when your last tenant checked out for which you had received rent up until, what costs are you actually incurring? Calculate this on a monthly basis like I've done for my property below:

- Mortgage: £290
- Council tax: £97
- Electricity: £45 (expected once bill received)
- Water: £25 (expected once bill received)
- Service charge: £190
- Ground rent: £25 (monthly pro-rated amount)
- Insurance: £13 (monthly pro-rated amount)
- Maintenance: £0 (paid by previous tenant's deposit)
- Estate agent fees: £0 (only pay when property is let)

**Total monthly cash outflow: £685**

£685! That's a lot of money I've got to pay out. Every. Single. Month. That works out to be £23 a day and a whopping £8,220 a year.

### 3.3.3.2 Calculate the Void "Opportunity Cost"

In property void terms, "Opportunity Cost" is a fancy way of saying, "What money am I missing out on by not having a tenant paying rent?" It's similar to the monthly calculation we did in Point 1, with a few differences that I'll explain using the same example:

- Lost rent: £900 (this is the rent I won't receive each month the property remains un-let)

- ~~Mortgage £290~~ (not applicable for opportunity cost as I pay this regardless of whether I have a tenant)
- Council tax: £97 (only pay this for void period, tenant pays when tenanted. There are some reductions for vacant property but let's ignore these to keep it simple)
- Electricity: £45 (only pay this for void period, tenant pays when tenanted)
- Water: £25 (only pay this for void period, tenant pays when tenanted)
- ~~Service charge: £190~~ (not applicable for opportunity cost as I pay this regardless of whether I have a tenant)
- ~~Ground rent: £25 (pro-rated)~~ (not applicable for opportunity cost as I pay this regardless of whether I have a tenant)
- ~~Insurance: £13 (pro-rated)~~ (not applicable for opportunity cost as I pay this regardless of whether I have a tenant)
- Maintenance: £0 (not applicable as no additional repairs from property being void)
- High street agent fees: -£135 (when property is let, I used to pay approx. 15%, or £135 to the high street agent, so I save on this cost when property is vacant)

**Total monthly opportunity cost: £932**

Remember, this is not what cash I'm actually paying out (that was Point 1). Instead, Point 2 is showing me what it's effectively costing me on a monthly basis by not having a tenant. It's a huge number. £31 a day. £11,184 a year. I need to find a tenant fast!

And here's where it gets interesting. This information allows me to re-assess the rental price I'm currently marketing the flat at.

It's normal for landlords to want to charge maximum rent for their property, and often, spurred on by valuations provided by high street agents, landlords will hold out for higher rents.

But is this a good idea in the long term? Take my property for example, let's say someone offered £850 a month. My gut tells me this is too low. I may even get a little annoyed··· how dare they value my flat at such a low value!

Well, actually, if I was to accept £850 rent a month and they moved in tomorrow, that would reduce my yearly profit by £510 vs if I waited and let the property out at £900 (12 months x (£900 – £850) x 0.85% to account for agent fees). That is roughly half of the £932 I lose each month for the property being void.

So, actually, unless I think I can let the property at £900 within two weeks' time, it's better to accept a lower rent of £850. Even shorter if we agreed a rental of £875, etc.

Obviously, you don't know how long it will take to let a property at a given price, but this technique does put you in a much better position to assess your expected rental amount.

**Key message**: Calculate how much a void actually costs you (cash outflow and opportunity cost). It doesn't need to be 100% perfect. Again, don't overthink these things. You just want a reasonable feel for what the number is. Use that information to better assess the rental price the flat is marketed at, as well as offers received below your expected valuation—a lower rental amount may actually save you money if you reduce your void period.

### 3.3.4 Tip 4: Don't be Afraid to Alter the Price

Have you listed your property and had no enquiries after a week? Or perhaps only a few lukewarm enquiries? Assuming the advert is live and the property isn't a total wreck, it's probably overpriced. Drop the price. Quickly. Try a new level. And feel free to keep trying new levels.

Conversely, if you list your property and have 50 phone calls/messages the following day all offering to rent your property that same day, you may have under-cooked it. No worries. In fact, I'd like to be in that situation. You'll have the enviable position of being able to choose the tenants you feel are the best fit for the property, and will likely have a minimal void period, and minimal work required to the property before they move in. You can also communicate to the applicants the high demand. Keen tenants are likely to raise their offer price accordingly.

What is just right? After listing has been live for a few days, you want to have received at least a few enquiries with prospective tenants pushing to view the property. Not hundreds, but at least a few.

*"The first time I listed my property, I thought I could get a much higher price. Despite no enquiries for eight days, I stubbornly stuck with that. With hindsight, I'd have reduced the price after just a few days." (Aaron, new landlord)*

**Key rent price-setting message:** Use the above tips to choose your starting point. But don't be afraid to adjust that. Be adaptable to the feedback you'll get within the first few days of listing.

Time to bust a myth:

Myth: "I don't know how much rent to charge."

BUSTED!

Selecting an appropriate rent to charge is not rocket science.

You now know many ways to work out what rent to charge to ensure you receive acceptable levels of income and the tenant is paying a fair amount of rent. You even know you can alter this based on the initial feedback you receive after listing the property online. This is an easy part of self-managing your rental property!

Take action and add the rental price to your online property profile.

## 3.4 Before You Hit "Submit"

Do your final checks and then your profile is complete and ready to upload. Before you hit that submit button, there are a few final points you need to complete.

### 3.4.1 Viewing Availability

Take a moment to consider your availability for viewings, as most online agents will require you to enter days and times that prospective tenants can then choose from.

The days/times you choose is entirely down to you and what works best for you. Naturally, you want to give prospective tenants as many options as possible, but there are a few things to consider:

- **Your current tenants:** Assuming your property is currently occupied, speak to the current tenants and ask nicely what days/times work best for them. Do your best to make these as hassle-free as possible for them (i.e. can you batch viewings in a certain slot to minimise constant disruptions?).

- **Your own schedule.** Don't offer up everything. While it's tempting to cater 100% for prospective tenants, as long as you give a reasonable number of slots tailored to your target tenants (i.e. professionals may want evenings after 6 pm, or lunch hours, etc.), you will get viewings. If you have a nice property marketed at a reasonable level, tenants will find a way to make one of the slots you offer up.

Remember, if it's not convenient for you, don't feel obliged. Our objective as self-managing landlords is to be as efficient as possible so that it takes up as little time as possible (remember the 25 hours I mentioned at the start of the book?).

Here's what I offer up:

- One weekday evening (5-8 pm)
- One lunch hour weekday slot (12-2 pm)
- Saturday late morning/early afternoon (11 am-3 pm)

*"I've only ever once had to do viewings on more than two different days/slots, which I've achieved by limiting the viewing availability and then liaising with tenants upfront to move their preferred ties around to better suit my schedule."*

Once I have viewings confirmed, I nearly always then move tenants around to better fit my schedule. I've never lost a tenant viewing for politely requesting this.

I arrange 15-minute intervals, and have found that some arrive late, some are early, and it doesn't matter either way. Sometimes it has meant I've had multiple tenants viewing the property at the same time. This helps create a buzz and feeling of "must act soon", which I like.

Finally, click submit. Please note it can take 24 hours(ish) for your property to be reviewed and then appear on the portals. You'll get a notification that it is LIVE. Be sure to double-check all the details are correct and don't be afraid to ask the online agent to make changes if something doesn't look right.

### 3.4.2 Uploading Documents to Your Online Agent

There are a few documents you can add to your online property profile. Some important, others not so much, but here's a few most online agents will allow you to upload:

- EPC – I'll explain what this is later, but definitely something to add as it will allow prospective tenants to see this when viewing the property online.
- Title deeds – non-essential but handy to store online.
- Electrical certificate.
- Gas certificate.

### 3.4.3 Social Media Advertising

But wait, even after advertising your property online, there is more you can (and should) do! Pretty sure you'll have heard of Facebook. Well, why not share the link to your property online? Even better, post it in groups (check with group owner first that this is permitted) that are likely to have your target market (in my above example, I post in Greenwich family groups, along with Canary Wharf professional groups to maximise the chances of reaching my target audience).

Well done for taking the first big step!

With that in mind, let's find out how to deal with the inevitable flurry of enquiries you are about to receive.

## 3.5 Chapter Summary

- To advertise your property online, you need to sign up with an online agent who will facilitate this for you along with managing tenant enquiries.
- Online agents charge significantly cheaper fees than high street agents, whilst offering a much more flexible service.
- It's important to upload good photos and a well written description to your property advert.
- There are many ways to find out how much rent to charge, and it's important to know the cost of a void before you do this.

# 4.0 CHOOSING TENANTS

If there is one thing that can make a huge difference to the quality of your life as a landlord, it's choosing the right tenants.

Choose well, and rent comes in, the day to day management is hassle-free and they stay for many years to come. Choose badly and, well... it's bad (I'll show you some of the issues in later chapters!). Don't worry, this is very infrequent, but you do want to give yourself the best chance of having good tenants.

Now, let's be totally honest here. There is an element of luck involved. No amount of research or referencing process is perfect, just as you can never judge what someone is like from just meeting them once. And people can even change!

So, all you can do is give yourself the best chance by making sure you follow some key steps (which, believe me, many landlords skip!). You'll find out how in this chapter.

*"I didn't bother to reference a new tenant as they seemed nice and wanted to move in ASAP, paying three months' rent upfront. Turns out that was the only rent payment they made during their 11-month stay in my property. I'm still trying to recoup my losses." (Jess, landlord, Brighton)*

## 4.1 Types of Tenant – Which Ones Are Right For You?

Before we go through the steps of managing viewings and screening tenants, let's think about types of tenant. Of course, there are many and tenants usually fit into more than one group, but having an idea of what groups there are, and which are well suited to your property, makes screening much easier.

Here's a non-exhaustive list—split into three main groups—and stating the obvious, but tenants could form any combination of the below broad groupings:

### 4.1.1 Who is Your Tenant?

- **Your friends/family.** Don't do it. Simple. It always seems like a good idea beforehand, yet rarely works out well and often ends up getting very messy. Your rental property is a business, so keep it professional, i.e. with a tenant where you are not personally involved in any way.

- **Families.** In whatever form families come. Single parents, hundreds of kids, etc. My preferred type of tenant. One thing to consider, if the prospective tenants have kids, is your property/area kid-friendly? Think about high balconies, busy roads, dangerous staircases, etc.

- **Single person.** Even in these modern times of smaller properties and people sharing to keep costs low, single people do still rent property. On their own. And that's probably how they like it. As it's just one person, make sure at the referencing stage they have sufficient income to cover the rent.

- **Couples.** Another favourite of mine. It usually works out cost-effective for a couple to share the rent. In general (and this is making a very broad assumption), I find them more likely to look after a property than a singleton or sharers. Perhaps they are less likely to party than singletons, or is that just me after I moved in with my wife?!

- **Sharers**. Two friends. A few friends. Two people who work together. So many possibilities. Personally, I prefer this setup less as I have found sharers are more likely to move out sooner (perhaps one wants to move in with a new partner, job moves, etc.). Don't let it put you off though.

### 4.1.2 What is Their Occupation?

Let's face it, this is quite an important area of your prospective tenants' life to know about as it's likely this profession will be the source of income from which your rent will get paid.

- **Employed**. Most common and easily my favourite. Ideally a stable job with regular/fixed paychecks where they have been employed for a while. Not that I'd necessarily discount someone who had worked there for less time—we are all allowed a job move! Without wanting to sound too snobby, I usually aim for working professionals as the properties I own are in areas that appeal to them. Personal preference and driven by my property type and location.

- **Self-employed.** Good on them. A business person like yourself. Slightly harder to reference but certainly not something I'd shy away from. Always good to understand what business they run, how long it's been operating for and check that it generates enough cash to pay your rent.

- **Students**. Yes, even students need a place to live. I've only let to students once, who used their parents as guarantors. Is your property in an area with lots of students, or close to a University campus? If so, it's worth considering student lets. Generally (and please don't take this as gospel), properties are not maintained to the same level, so you are looking at lower rents, lower-quality properties here.

- **Those on benefits**. The benefits system is a whole big topic within itself, and not one I want to delve into detail in this book. Are you willing to rent to someone on benefits? I have, and still do. Some might argue it's riskier, but I always consider each applicant on their own merits. Your tenant in this scenario could be a council, housing association or even charitable organisation on behalf of the tenant.

- **Company lets**. A company could look to rent your property. Perhaps a business nearby wishes to house one of their employees who is moving to the area. They would be your tenant and named on the legal agreement.

Be aware that some companies will offer to be your tenant and will then find tenants to live in your property. Usually, lots of tenants as they take a spread on rents they receive vs what they pay you. Rent-to-rent as it's known. This setup can work, but do your homework to make sure they are reputable, and don't be fooled into thinking their "guaranteed" rent promise is 100% safe—unless they pay all of it upfront, of course.

### 4.1.3 Other Tenant Attributes

There's a few other things to think about as well:

- **Pets**. Do you love pets? If so, you are more likely to allow tenants to have pets in your property. However, even if you do love those cute adorable fluffy things, you may choose not to allow them as they usually bring with them more wear and tear (sofa scratches, dog hair, noise, etc.).

- **Smokers**. As a non-smoker, for me, this is a big no. You can instantly tell if a property has a smoker living there, and the smoke smell is almost impossible to fully get out of carpets, curtains, etc. Smoker landlords are more likely to consider smokers. Up to you.

- **Disability.** Is your property suitable for someone with a disability? More on the legal aspects later, but for now, just be aware that some prospective tenants may have a disability (remember, this may not be obvious/visible) and you want your property to be as accommodating as possible.

- **Nationality**. Prospective tenants may be from the UK or from overseas—or a mix of those two. Let's be clear, landlords should never discriminate on nationality, or anything else for that matter. But it is important to be aware of your tenants' nationality as there are legal considerations to follow here. I'll cover these later in—yep, you've guessed it—the legal section.

There are many more pros and cons for each type of tenant, and what is right for you is unique to each individual property and your own preferences.

Use common sense and just be aware of some of the different types and attributes when you do the viewings and market your property.

## 4.2 Screening Tenants and Managing Viewings

It's getting real now. You've set the right price, uploaded the property profile to the portals, provided your availability and now the viewing requests come in by text and email—see example for one of my properties below sent to me by my online agent:

*"You have a new appointment request for 2.30 pm on Saturday 27/03/2021 at Property Address. Reply 100000 CONFIRM to accept this or* https://www.makeurmove.co.uk/viewing/update/100000 *to amend."*

Can you make that slot? Simply reply back via text with "100000 CONFIRM". If not, log in and provide a revised time slot. Even if I can't make that particular slot, I usually accept. By doing this, you are provided with the tenants' contact details. I then reach out directly to find a mutually convenient time slot.

Before any viewing, I like to pre-screen tenants by way of a 5-10-minute introductory call. This is beneficial to me and the tenant as it's a good way of ensuring the property is suitable for them before going there in person, thus potentially saving both parties a lot of time.

*"Initially, I found that approximately half of tenants never showed up to appointments. By pre-screening tenants and keeping in touch with reminders prior to their visit, it's very rare now that I don't have a tenant turn up at the time they are expected."*

Yes, it does take up more of your precious time (not much!) in the short term, but only conducting viewings to suitable and interested tenants saves significantly more time in the long term. Tenants who are keen will be happy to take the call. Any who don't respond or are not happy to take the call are unlikely to attend on the day. Do this and save yourself a wasted visit to your property—nothing is more frustrating than that.

Here's an example text message I send to the tenant to set this up:

*"Hi NAME, hope you are well. My name is Louis Bamberger and I am the landlord of PROPERTY ADDRESS. Thank you for expressing an interest in the property. I look forward to seeing you on DAY/TIME. Before the viewing, are you free for a quick call where I can quickly to tell you about the property and answer any upfront questions you have? Thanks, Louis."*

I never say this is an interview or that I want to ask them questions as I feel that is too intimidating/unfair on them. Instead, I want them to feel this is for their benefit (which it also is!) and will then ask my questions more subtly once we are talking. Here's how I do it once we've arranged a time for the call:

1) Warmly introduce myself. Thank them for their time and for expressing an interest.

2) Give high level details on the property. Include even basic details such as where it is, how many bedrooms and what the rent is. You'll be amazed at how many people have forgotten these simple things, or are confusing it with other properties they are viewing. Mention when it's available, details of furnishings, parking, etc. And yes, obviously mention good features or benefits!

Here's where you can glean information from them in a subtle way. As you go through the property, flip points back to them. Here's a few examples of how to do it:

- The property has say two bedrooms. Ask them if it's just them or do they have family/friends who will be living in the property? Do they have pets, etc.?

- The property is say in Greenwich, London. Do they know the area well? Will they be travelling in from far? Will it be close to where they work? (See what I'm doing here?!)

- The property is unfurnished. Does the place they are living in now have furniture? When are they looking to move? Do they have a car to help move their belongings?

The list is endless. I'm sure you can think of other questions that will allow you to glean useful information at this point.

You don't have to gather everything here, so keep it light and don't worry if there is some of the above info you can't obtain naturally. You'll have another chance when you meet them in person, and then there are formal references to check employment income/credit checks, etc.

Answer any questions they have. It's important to tell the truth here. While you want to sell the property, you don't want to mislead them, only to have them disappointed on the day, and you waste your time on an un-necessary viewing. I've told prospective tenants of a one-bed flat of mine that I don't think it was suitable as the property was small for a family of four. Telling them anything differently would be a waste of everyone's time.

*"I spoke to a prospective tenant once who was interested in my small one-bed flat in Maidenhead. It was for himself and three other family members. I decided to be honest upfront about the size of the flat, after which he said it would be too small. I'm glad we found this out on a two-minute phone call, rather than meeting at the property itself for a viewing."*

At the end of the call, thank them and explain the next steps, namely that you'll see them on DAY/TIME. Give any instructions on what to do when they arrive, like ring a buzzer or call your mobile.

I also drop in briefly how it would work if they make an offer that is accepted, and always drop in casually that references will be done to look at previous address history, credit checks and employment income. I don't like formally asking them if there are issues here, but informally letting them know this is part of the process should deter unwanted tenants or encourage them to raise issues early—which you can then discreetly steer clear of.

Some may say this is overkill, but the day before I send them a standard text reminder, and the same again on the day itself. Regular and clear communication takes so little time, but has the potential to save me hours of wasted time.

Finally, I would just note that not all tenants will have the same efficiency and responsiveness as you. They can be good tenants but with poor communication skills. They may not reply to any messages and turn up on the day. Not often, but it can happen.

However, in most cases, keen and good tenants reply quickly and are happy to engage in a pre-viewing chat.

## 4.3 Viewings – On the Day

Are you excited? Today you get to meet prospective tenants and showcase why they should want to rent your property. Hopefully, you have a number of appointments set up around the same time, and know they will be attending because you've checked in with them on numerous occasions.

First things first. Get there early! Nothing is worse than arriving late as it sends tenants a very bad message. It's also important to ensure you have time beforehand to prepare the property so they see it in its best light.

I always start by opening windows to freshen the air. If the property is cold, turn the heating on to make it more appealing. These small details can make a difference.

Lights should be turned on. No one wants to see a poorly lit property because you are trying to save a few pennies on electricity. Warm, cosy, well-lit properties will entice tenants so much more.

Tidy or re-arrange furniture to bring out the most in a room. If you are feeling fancy, why not bring some flowers to give the property that extra special feel. Or set out a bottle of wine and some glasses on a table. You are selling a home to a tenant. You want them to easily be able to picture just how nice it will be living there. Use your imagination.

As a self-managing landlord, you sometimes need to get your hands dirty. Literally. Bring cleaning items, including wipes, disinfectant spray, air freshener, bleach for the toilets, etc.

*"I don't suggest you do a full deep clean yourself (pay professionals for that), but even clean flats I like to spruce up a bit with a 10-min whizz of cleaning."*

When they first walk in, I want the property to smell nice and clean. I'd also suggest bringing toilet rolls and bin bags.

Remembering the keys also helps!

Now think about yourself. Remember, as a landlord, you are also a business owner. I'd recommend dressing reasonably smartly as those first impressions count both ways.

When you first meet tenants, greet them warmly and politely. A smile goes a long way.

Small talk is a good thing. Unless you have hundreds of viewings lined up, don't feel the need to rush straight in to showing them around. Ask questions, talk about yourself. Build that relationship. Did they find it ok? Take them long to get there? Do they know the area well?

Then offer to show them around. I say "offer" because sometimes I've found that tenants like to look around on their own, then come to you for questions after. Whatever works.

I like to give them a high-level overview first; i.e. it's a two-bedroom flat with an en-suite, open-plan kitchen diner and balcony.

This may be overkill again, but I like to start with the **second**-best room in the property, then go through each room, pointing out benefits and key features. Don't be afraid to sell these. If there is a dishwasher, show them. If the painting has just been re-done, tell them. Heated towel rails, yes please!

I also don't shy away from any negative points. It's best to address these upfront so you can control the dialogue, highlighting why it's not a huge issue. If the second bedroom is tiny, it will be obvious, so reference it, and then mention how it's ideal as an office or storage space. Building works on their way in? Mention when they are due to finish so tenants know it's only temporary.

*"One of my properties is right next to a busy railway station. I reference this early on and mention that the flat is doubled glazed so it can't be heard and that previous tenants with a baby had no issues. I then mention that train provides excellent transport connections, and did they know it only takes eight minutes to XYZ? A potential negative is quickly turned into a positive."*

I always end the "tour" in the best room or next to the best feature. It's here that they will likely ask questions and discuss the property in more detail, including admin such as utilities, when it's vacant, etc. Might as well have them standing next to the feature they most likely want when you have these conversations!

Ask them what they think. How does it compare to others they are viewing? All feedback is good feedback and will allow you to improve your offering.

On their way out, make sure you discuss what the next steps are if they are interested, and invite further questions over text or phone. Here's what I send:

*"Really nice to meet you earlier, NAME. Let me know if you have any questions about the property or would like to make an offer on the property. Many thanks, Louis."*

My best story here was one tenant who liked it so much she asked me to help her make the offer online using her phone whilst we were stood in the property. Result!

Here's a few other important points to consider:

1) **Safety** – Will it just be you in the property on the day? Whilst it's unlikely you will encounter any difficulties (especially as you will have already spoken to the prospective tenant to screen them over the phone), if possible, have someone else with you to help, or at least nearby—just in case.

1) **Security** – Does your property have any valuable items in it? If so, be sensible. Don't leave items out on display and do your best to be in the same room as your prospective tenants at all times. If you have current tenants, it's likely they will (quite righty) insist on this. Theft is unlikely, as long as you use common sense.

3) Be **organised** – If many prospective tenants are visiting on the same day, keep a list of people's names, and note any defining features or information about them to help you remember them. It's very easy to forget!

For all of the three above points, having a second person with you when you do these viewings makes life a lot easier!

Might just be me, but I find this a really enjoyable part of being a landlord. You get to meet people and talk about property. Approach viewings with this "fun" mindset and I think you'll end up loving it like I do.

## 4.4 Negotiating & Choosing Offers

Hopefully, after a few viewings, you will have an offer or two. Sometimes these will be given formally through the online agent but can be informal negotiation via text first.

Offers can range from a good prospective tenant offering the full asking price with minimal requests, to those asking for a significant discount or with conditions attached.

Which brings us to negotiation. Whilst this is not a book on negotiation (Donald Trump has written one of these if you are interested), there are a few property-specific items I'd like to draw your attention to:

- **Keep discussions friendly and fair** (you are a business owner, so act professionally).

- **Don't take things personally.** Other people won't have the emotional ties that you have to the property. They will naturally value it less than you and may pick up on negative points. This is fine, it's just negotiation/business.

- **Don't quibble over tiny details**, you lose goodwill. Does it really matter if a tenant wants to move in four days later, or wants the property cleaned first?

- **Give and take** – Don't worry about conceding points, you can likely make them up elsewhere.

- **Best business relationships in the long term are those that work well for BOTH parties**··· not just one/you!

There are likely a number of points you'll be discussing during the negotiating or even choosing between offers. Here are the key ones:

- Rental amount offered

- Proposed move-in date/contract length

- Any furniture/maintenance requirements

- Tenants themselves (impressions, occupation, etc.)

Don't fall into the trap of basing the majority of your decision on rental income offered. Rookie landlord error that. There is a cost/risk associated to all of the above items—you don't need to have a Maths PhD to calculate perfectly the impact of each, but you need to at least be aware and have a rough idea.

Here's an example to illustrate this:

Offer 1

- Rent £1,600 per month
- Move in ASAP
- 12-month contract
- Professional clean required

Offer 2

- Rent £1,700 per month
- Move in two months from now
- 6-month contract
- New sofa requested

Offer 2 to the untrained eye might seem more appealing. £100 a month more rent is a lot more. But you need to consider the other factors. However, if Offer 1 tenant can move in ASAP (let's say two weeks' time to factor in referencing/contracts), then that is 1.5 months earlier than Offer 2. Which is a difference of 1.5 months x £1,600 rent = £2,400. So, that costs you a lot more as you'll recall from the earlier section on calculating the cost of a void period.

Contract length is also a factor. You want tenants to stay longer. it reduces the number of inevitable voids you have between tenants. So, I try to avoid six-month contracts if possible. This should not be the key consideration but just something to be aware of.

I also try not to be overly swayed by smaller items like tenant requests to replace a sofa or have the property professionally cleaned. But they can help you make a decision if all other things are equal.

Finally, think about the calibre of tenant. How did they seem to you? What is their source of income? Do they seem reliable? You don't have a crystal ball here, but factoring in their suitability to be long-term tenants helps.

Just remember, there is unlikely to ever be the "perfect" offer, each will have their pros and cons. You will never have full or perfect information when making this decision. Use the information you have, the knowledge above and you can make a calculated and confident decision.

### 4.1.1 Offer Accepted – What Next?

Congratulations. You are ready to accept an offer. It's as simple as logging in to your online agent account and pressing "accept".

The tenant will receive the notification that their offer has been accepted, and will be required to pay a holding deposit of one weeks' rent to fully secure the property (i.e. to have it taken off the market). You get notified once this has been paid, and the property is taken offline while referencing is underway. Any future viewings are automatically cancelled.

The online agent will also kick-start the referencing (if you request it) and draft contracts for your review.

## 4.5 Referencing – Get it Right

Referencing is a vital part of being a landlord and this deserves a separate section. I cannot emphasise just how important this is. It can cost you additional money with some online agents (for lots, including Makeurmove, it's no extra charge, however), approximately £15-20 per person, but it is a cost that must not be skipped.

One of the biggest landlord worries (myths) about self-managing their property is that they will choose a bad tenant who won't pay them rent, or will trash their property.

Well, by referencing your tenant, you can give yourself the best chance of preventing this from happening. So, read on…

You might also be thinking, "I don't know how to do this, surely only a high street agent can properly reference tenants?" Wrong.

Referencing is incredibly simple and can be done easily by anyone online. I'd recommend you use the same online agent who have marketed your property to undertake these, as with a few easy clicks, they will set this up for you. Note: They don't do it themselves, they outsource it to a professional referencing company. Doing it this way is exactly the same process as high street agents follow.

You can also shop around and get a marginally cheaper deal by contacting professional referencing companies yourself. For example, the NRLA offer reasonably priced reference services to members. With Makeurmove, their "Good Landlord" package includes references for two tenants. Cheap as chips.

References cover a number of key items to validate the tenant as best as possible, including:

### 4.5.1 What Information You Get From Referencing

- **Identity verification.** Check they are who they say they are. Name, age, etc.

- **Affordability**. Can they realistically afford to rent your property? Common sense works best here. If they earn £25,000 a year, and the annual rent is £18,000, after tax, can they pay their rent and other living expenses? Nope. Everyone seems to have a different formula to back up common sense, but if you start with making sure their annual salary is 2.5x higher than the annual rent, you won't go too far wrong.

- **Income verification.** Don't just take a tenants' word for how much they earn and where they work. The referencing company will check this is actually the case by getting confirmation from an employer or from payslips or electronic banking clever means that validate this. They will also look at their contract length and how long they've worked there. You'll also find out whether they have a work permit or appropriate work visa if need be.

> A pro tip is to request the contact details for the last TWO landlords. The last landlord may be biased into saying they are a good tenant, just to get rid of them! The landlord before that should be able to give an unbiased view. Not essential, but good to know about.

- **Address history.** References provide useful info such as where they live now and have been linked with previously. Useful for ensuring their "story" adds up, and you can go further and request their previous landlord's contact details and ask for a reference if you have any doubts.

- **Credit rating.** Important one. Includes whether they have any County Court Judgements ("CCJs") or Bankruptcies in their name. Be extremely cautious if items show up here. In my opinion (so not always the case, I'm not perfect, remember!), someone who has allowed themselves to get into financial difficulty before is far more likely to do so again. I personally don't want that extra risk.

- **Guarantor.** If you need to use a guarantor to get your tenants to pass referencing, they will also need to be referenced with you getting the same information on them as above for your actual tenants.

- **Self-employment.** Linked to income verification but harder for those who are self-employed, especially those who operate on a cash basis. Referencing can help check bank statements and tax returns. Some extra digging your side can be done here.

PRO LANDLORD TIP: Use the power of social media to aid your referencing. Nowadays, nearly all tenants will have a social media presence. Spend 10 minutes searching online, looking at LinkedIn (job details), Facebook and even Google in case they appear on other pages.

This sounds a bit of a creepy stalky thing to do, but anything you find will be in public domain, and may just give you a slightly better feel for the type of person they really are—and whether they are suitable for your property. See lots of anti-social aggressive Facebook rants or drunken party photos? Maybe not who you want.

No need to get snobby here, we've all probably got social media photos we don't know are posted or should take down, but no harm in trying to get that extra bit of intel on your tenants before it's too late!

Anyway, that's why and what you get from referencing. If you follow my advice and use your online agent, this will be done for you with minimal effort or stress needed from you.

How long do they take? The speed you receive the completed reports depends on how quick the tenant is to provide the information (or their employer). I find they normally take at least a few days, maybe a week. Going back a few years, they seemed to take multiple weeks. The world has sped up since then.

### 4.5.2 Making a Decision on Referencing Reports

One of the many things I love about online agents and being a self-managing landlord is that you are closer to your property business, and when it comes to referencing, this means that you get a copy of the reference reports.

The reports usually have a very clear "pass" or "fail" recommendation, which I often find to be enough in making a decision on their acceptability. The full details then take a few pages which you can read in a few minutes. Pretty simple stuff.

A "pass" recommendation and quick skim of the info should be enough to proceed, which, hey presto, can be done by clicking a button saying something along the lines of "accept references and proceed to contract."

Please note, you don't have to accept a "pass" reference, or reject a "fail" reference. The decision is yours. You are in control here.

*"I have on occasions reached out to the tenant where I feel more information is required. For example, I had a self-employed tenant where I wanted to know a bit more about the income that the references provided. I also asked for a letter from the previous landlord once, where I felt less sure so I wanted to gain more assurance on their suitability."*

Don't feel you have to know everything about this tenant from the last 10 years. That is not realistic or fair. This is a process whereby you reduce your risk, but it's impossible to eliminate the risk. It's an important part of a landlords' mindset to accept that.

There are also some occasions where a "fail" may not mean they are rejected. As a tenant myself, I've been "failed" on referencing before as my move was during a career break where I had no income. However,

I was eventually accepted as I was able to demonstrate via bank statements that I had sufficient cash to cover the 12 months' rent.

I've also had a current tenant fail her referencing due to having moved to the UK recently and not having a previous address history or credit rating. Rather than a "computer says no" approach, I consider each situation for its own merits and risk and make a calculated decision.

Also, some "fails" are because the income is deemed insufficient to meet the rent, but a guarantor is provided. I'm fine with this as long as the guarantor checks out.

Just remember, running a business (rental property) comes with risks. This is one way to help you reduce those risks, and therefore, sleep better at night. Be sensible and don't skip this part of the process.

Once the references are received, and assuming acceptable, you then get the option online to "approve", which allows the agent to initiate the paperwork.

It's time to bust a myth…

> Myth: "I'm worried I'll choose a bad tenant who will trash my property or won't pay me rent!"
>
> 
>
> BUSTED!
>
> This was one of my biggest worries before switching to self-managing my properties.
>
> Until I realised that the risk of this happening could be significantly reduced by performing detailed reference checks on prospective tenants. Even better, these reference reports are extremely easy to obtain and review, allowing you to make an informed decision on letting to a tenant.
>
> What's more, collecting a deposit (something we'll cover in the next chapter) reduces your risk even more. Don't let this unnecessary worry put you off of self-managing!

This brings us nicely onto the legal aspects on being a landlord. Grab yourself a coffee.

## 4.6 Chapter Summary

- It's important to know about the different types of tenant, along with details of their occupation and other attributes.
- Save time by pre-screening tenants with a short phone call before the viewing.
- Managing tenant viewing appointments can be done easily through your online agent portal.
- On the day itself, make sure you are well prepared. First impressions count!
- Negotiation is a process all landlords go through, and it doesn't have to be stressful.
- Referencing tenants is essential for landlords, and very easy to complete.

# 5.0 LEGAL ASPECTS

Legal aspects are what often deter landlords from making the switch to self-management.

It's another landlord worry (myth) that they won't have the necessary legal skillset to draw up tenancy agreements and ensure compliance with the myriad of property regulations if they switch to self-managing.

This is simply not true. Anyone with half a brain can quickly learn the minimum information required to ensure you run your property rental business in accordance with the relevant and property rules and regulations.

And even better, you don't need to be a lawyer or even have to draft these documents yourself. They are all readily available online.

Use this chapter to understand what rules are out there, and then importantly find out how you can easily and cheaply ensure you comply with these.

I won't lie, this chapter is a biggie, so break it up in sections. A checklist of the different rules is also added to the final chapter to make life easier for you.

*"I'm rubbish at paperwork and any legal/admin forms, so the thought of drafting a tenancy agreement myself terrified me. Luckily, I now know how easy these are to get right!" (Emma, Surrey landlord)*

## 5.1 Tenancy Agreements

You'd have to have been born on another planet to not know that tenancy agreements are the bedrock of property rental. You should never let your property without a tenancy agreement in place. NEVER!

Ok, I'll stop shouting. Let's start simple. What is a tenancy agreement?

> A **tenancy agreement** is a contract between the landlord and the tenant which sets out in writing all the terms and conditions of the tenancy. This includes things like how long the tenancy will last, how much rent the landlord expects the tenant to pay, and when these payments are due.

Like any other contract, it is legally binding, and if either party breaches the contract, there are consequences. Cue scary music...

While that may sound ominous, it really is just common sense. If you agree to something with someone, best to write it down, hey? Property rental is no different.

But let's be clear. You don't have to have a tenancy agreement in place to let a property or room to a tenant, although you'd be a numpty if you thought this was a good idea.

It's important to note before we look at the types of tenancy agreement available and what goes into them, that as soon as a tenant pays you rent, a tenancy is deemed to have been created under the Law of Property Act 1925. This means you have the same statutory duties as the 99.9% of landlords who do have a tenancy agreement in place.

This means that tenants automatically have certain rights, including to:

- Live in a property that's safe and in a good state of repair.
- Have their deposit returned when the tenancy ends, and in some circumstances, have it protected.
- Challenge excessively high charges.
- Know who their landlord is and where they live.
- Live in the property undisturbed.
- See an Energy Performance Certificate for the property.
- Be protected from unfair eviction and unfair rent.

All pretty fair, common sense stuff.

So, let's get down to business. There are a few types of tenancy agreement, and all you need is a basic understanding of what these are (hint: you probably only need to read about the first one).

### 5.1.1 Types of Tenancy Agreement

#### Assured shorthold tenancies ("ASTs")

This is by far the most common form of tenancy agreement. Most new tenancies are this type as a tenancy is automatically an AST unless it is explicitly stated otherwise.

A tenancy can be an AST if all of the following apply:

- The property you rent out is private (obviously).
- The tenancy started on or after 15 January 1989 (I was barely born then).
- The property is the tenant's main accommodation (likely).
- You, the landlord, do not live in the property (hope not).
- The rent is less than £100,000 a year (I wish).

- The rent is more than £250 a year, or more than £1,000 in London (bit cheap).
- It's not a business tenancy, licensed premises or holiday let and your tenant is not a local council.

Let's assume you will be letting under an AST. There are then three types of AST to be aware of:

- **Fixed-term** – Running for a set period of time as the name suggests, typically for six or 12 months. You can't raise the rent during this time unless the tenant agrees, or there's a rent review clause in the contract.
- **Periodic tenancy** – Running on a week-by-week or month-by-month basis, the tenancy rolls on for an indefinite period.
- **Statutory periodic tenancy** – When the initial fixed-term has ended and the landlord hasn't agreed to a new fixed-term with the tenant. Put simply, once the fixed-term is over, if you don't sign a new contract with your tenant, the tenancy agreement automatically becomes 'periodic', moving in most cases to a monthly rolling contract with the same rent.

Here's my guess. You'll rent to your tenant on a fixed-term AST. Simples.

But do read on, just in case this doesn't apply as there are other tenancies that are not as common as ASTs, including:

### Assured tenancies

Tenancies starting between 15 January 1989 and 27 February 1997 may be assured. Tenants have increased protection from eviction with this type of agreement. Unlikely, given how old your tenancy would have to be.

### Non-assured shorthold tenancy

This type of tenancy can only be used in particular situations, where an assured shorthold tenancy can't be used. This may be because the rent is less than £250 per year, the tenant has their main home elsewhere, or you live in the same property as your tenant (as long as you don't share any facilities). Again, this is unlikely to apply to most.

### Regulated tenancies

Tenancies starting before 15 January 1989 may be regulated. This gives tenants increased protection from eviction and they can apply for a 'fair rent', potentially reducing what rent you can charge. Unless you are a dinosaur, this probably won't apply to you.

### Excluded tenancies, licences or lodger agreements

You may have an excluded tenancy, licence or lodger agreement if the tenant lodges with you and shares rooms with you, like a kitchen or bathroom. This is outside the scope of this book, but in a nutshell, the tenant will have fewer rights and you will be able to evict them with a court order.

### Holiday lets

This applies when you let your property for a few days or weeks at a time (think Airbnb). You don't need a formal tenancy agreement for this type of arrangement. Rules do still apply though, which you should check before embarking on this type of letting.

### Company lets

If you're renting your property to a company rather than an individual, the tenancy isn't an assured shorthold tenancy.

This means that it's not governed by the same rules when it comes to things like deposit protection and eviction, and you can give a 'notice to quit' to end the tenancy, rather than serving a Section 21 or Section 8 Notice.

Ok, so now you know the types of tenancy agreement out there. What do these agreements actually include then, I hear you ask?

### 5.1.2 What's in a Tenancy Agreement?

A basic tenancy agreement should include the following:

- The names and contact details of all people involved (landlord, tenant and potentially guarantor).
- The rental price and how and when it's paid.
- Information on how and when the rent will be reviewed.
- The deposit amount and how it will be protected.
- Details of when the deposit can be fully or partly withheld (for example, to repair damage you've caused).
- The property address.
- The start and end date of the tenancy.
- Any tenant or landlord obligations.
- An outline of bills you're responsible for.
- It can also include information on:
- Whether the tenancy can be ended early and how this can be done (i.e. a break clause).
- Who's responsible for minor repairs (other than those that the landlord is legally responsible for).
- Whether the property can be let to someone else (sublet) or have lodgers.

And to state the obvious, the terms of the tenancy agreement must be fair and comply with the law, and cannot have anything in it that may indirectly discriminate against the tenant.

*"I always add a six-month break clause to new 12-month fixed-term contracts, it just gives me peace of mind." (Leah, Tooting landlord)*

Finally, it's worth noting that if there is more than one person (tenant) named on the AST, then they are jointly and severally liable. Which means that if one doesn't pay, you have recourse to claim against the other for this amount. Not a likely scenario, but worth knowing about.

A section of the rules surrounding tenancy agreements is enough to put any landlord to sleep. So, let's bring it back to basics by stating the reality that the majority of tenancies will fall under the AST fixed-term category, with some then moving onto the statutory periodic category when the initial fixed-term expires.

Ready to start drafting your legal contract? Worried you can't? Don't sweat!

### 5.1.3 How to Draft a Tenancy Agreement

You don't need to be a qualified lawyer to write or fully understand every bit of wording in the tenancy agreement. Instead, you just need to know where you can get hold of a well worded and legally enforceable tenancy agreement. That's the important part.

And here's the really good news. Your online agent will already have one of these. It will most likely come as part of the package you have signed up to. And even better, it will all be done electronically, saving you having to chop a tree or two down.

They will have example tenancy agreements for you to review on their website, so take a quick look. I've used the standard contracts of both Makeurmove and Openrent and have found both to be absolutely fine.

However, you don't have to use the online agent's standard contract. Instead, you can draft it yourself (not recommended), download from the NRLA (good choice) or research and download one online (I personally wouldn't).

When it comes to tenancy agreements, it really doesn't have to be complicated.

Let's say you decide to use the online agent's contract (well done, good choice). Remember that what's in the contract is not set in stone, so you can amend the terms if you need to. I'd advise against making any major alterations as I feel these are unlikely to be needed, but you may wish to add certain classes relevant to your own property. For example:

- Break clause (i.e. six months)
- Notice period if non-standard
- Any requirements re cleaning/gardening

The tenant needs to be comfortable signing this as well, so any alternations to the standard document should be made clear to them upfront. There is no element of trying to trick or hide anything here. You want everything laid out simply and fairly.

Electronic signing makes life so much easier. A few clicks of a button allows you to sign and also receive notifications once the tenant has signed their side. A copy is automatically sent to your email for you to save down. Technology has made life as a landlord so much more efficient. Use it.

It's time to bust a myth…

> Myth: "I don't know how to draft a tenancy agreement."
>
> BUSTED!
>
> I was so worried about getting the wording of my tenancy agreements wrong when I started self-managing my properties. Until I realised just how easy they are to complete.
>
> Because… you can get a perfectly worded tenancy agreement including within your package when you list with an online agent. You can also get fantastic templates online. For free. They even allow electronic signatures to save some trees. Tenancy agreements can be one of the easiest areas of being a self-managing landlord.

## 5.2 Collecting and Registering Tenant Deposits

Once the tenancy agreement is signed, the next step is for the tenant to pay a deposit. Before we consider the practical steps, let's take a step back and look at the concept of tenant deposits.

Deposits represent an amount paid by a tenant to a landlord at the outset of a tenancy and are typically equivalent to one month's rent—occasionally more. They are designed to cover such things as damage to a property, cleaning and unpaid utility bills or rent. It gives the landlord some downside risk protection, and incentivises the tenant to look after the property during their stay.

That sounds good, right? Pretty fair if you ask me.

In theory, yes. However, in the bad old days, some landlords would demand a hefty deposit from tenants, then return only a fraction of the deposit at the expiration of the tenancy, citing 'wear and tear' to the property, even if the properties were maintained to a high standard and rent was paid on time.

And the tenants, with limited government protection, in many cases, would just have to grin and bear it and suffer this unfair cost. That is not good. I've been a tenant myself on the receiving end of that, and it was horrible. Not how things should work.

Fear not. The residential property market is in a better place now though. Thanks to compulsory deposit schemes introduced by the government, the deposit system is far more transparent and fair to both parties these days.

### 5.2.1 Government-Backed Deposit Schemes

Landlords who collect a deposit from a tenant (and let's not forget, you don't have to request one—although I can't see why you wouldn't want to reduce your downside risk!) are legally required to safeguard their tenants' deposits with one of three government-backed deposit protection schemes:

*https://www.depositprotection.com/*

*https://www.mydeposit's.co.uk/*

*https://www.tenancydeposit'scheme.com/*

This legislation applies to all properties let on an assured shorthold tenancy agreement (and you know what one of those is now!) and applies throughout the tenancy term. No ifs, no buts. You must register your tenants' deposit in accordance with the rules.

How do these wonderful government deposit schemes actually work, I hear you shout loudly?

I'm glad you asked! These government schemes have the authority to govern tenancy deposits and oversee the process of deposit returns, deductions and disputes.

What this really does is stop landlords having the power to make an unfair judgement call on what deposit should be returned to a tenant. You, as the landlord, make the call on what you feel is appropriate to deduct from the tenants' deposit, but then an independent government scheme makes sure this is fair.

Let's face it. Even landlords (and I'm talking about you and me here) with the best intentions of acting fairly, naturally have a bias towards protecting their business and own personal finances. Bias never promotes fairness.

*"I learnt the rules the hard way when I first let out my property, deducting extra amounts from the tenants' deposit as a buffer for items potentially not picked up in the inventory. The tenant disputed this and I had to pay it all back, and got a slap on the wrists. I now know not to do this!" (Chris, London landlord)*

So, these tenancy deposit protection schemes provide tenants with added security and peace of mind. The schemes offer a faster, cheaper and fairer way of settling any disputes over the return of deposits, which is a great thing for landlords and tenants.

So, yeah, the schemes are kind of a big deal. In a good way.

Let's drill into this further. So, there are two basic types of deposit protection schemes. These are custodial and insurance.

### 5.2.2 Types of Deposit Scheme

Under the **custodial scheme**, the landlord lodges the deposit for the duration of the tenancy with the scheme provider. The money is then released to the tenant when the landlord and tenant have agreed how much of the original deposit should be repaid. In simple terms, the deposit is held by the custodial scheme (i.e. the cash is not in your bank account).

Under the second **insurance scheme**, the landlord pays a fee to have the deposit protected but keeps the money in their own account, then repays the tenant at the end of the tenancy. If the landlord fails to do so, the insurer will pay the tenant directly, then try to recoup the money from the landlord.

Which one should you do? Honestly, I don't think it matters. I have a slight preference for the custodial scheme as the online agent will send and register the money directly with the scheme—meaning I don't have to do anything, and don't have to keep a tenants' deposits segregated in a different personal bank account. It's less work for me. And I like doing less work. But I've also used the insurance schemes before. Both schemes work. Both offer the tenant protection. Whatever you prefer.

### 5.2.3 Other Rules Around Deposit Registration

Let's get nerdy for a second. When it comes to deposits, there's even more Ts and Cs, I'm afraid:

- Even if a deposit is paid by a third party (perhaps the tenant's parents), a full deposit protection scheme is still required by law. Simple rule: Collect a deposit. Register it.

- Registering the deposit must be done within 30 days from when you receive it. I'm sure you'll do it straight away.

- The landlord must give the tenant (and anyone who has paid the deposit for them, such as an employer or kind parents) certain required information (the "prescribed information"). Sounds tricky, but in reality, it's simple. When you register the deposit, the scheme will send you this automatically.

*"Your online agent will automatically send the prescribed information to the tenant by email, but I always forward this to the tenant myself, and ask them to confirm receipt of the email to be 100% sure they have received it."*

- A maximum of five weeks' rent can be collected (unless property income exceeds £50,000 per annum). Worth noting, I've never let out a property without requiring a tenant to pay anything less than the maximum five weeks' rent as a deposit. I'd strongly recommend you do the same.

Feel a bit overwhelmed, to the extent you are tempted to skip this requirement?

Don't. Because it's a) really not hard to comply when you use an online agent, and b) you open yourself up to getting absolutely shafted...

Should a tenant find out that a landlord hasn't protected their deposit, they can lodge a complaint with their local court. At this point, a court may order the landlord to repay the deposit to the tenant or place the deposit into a protection scheme within 14 days. That doesn't sound too bad, right? Just wait for it...

The court may also rule that the landlord has to pay up to three times the value of the deposit to the tenant as compensation. Wow! That's big. Not something I'd want for failing to do such a simple task.

What's more, failing to protect a deposit could also make it more difficult to evict a tenant under Section 21 of the Housing Act. We'll be covering evictions later, but trust me, this final point has the potential to be the most painful of the lot.

### 5.2.4 How to Actually Get a Deposit Registered

This all sounds very scary and daunting. A common landlord fear when it comes to self-managing. How could you possible ensure you comply with these complicated and potentially risky rules?

The answer, as it often is with residential property, is that it is really easy. Just by using an online agent means you will automatically be assisted in complying with this. Take the flat I've let earlier today as I'm writing this section (honestly!). Makeurmove collected the deposit, registered it and sent the tenant the prescribed information by email. It really is that simple.

You don't even have to use an online agent. You can even register tenants' deposits yourself (yes, that involves you having to do some work!). Use one of the links for government deposit schemes I added above, create an account, etc. It's more work so it won't get my personal recommendation, but it can be done.

Whatever you do, please just make sure you abide by the rules as the potential costs for not doing so are very severe.

And how about making sure we comply with the rules on returning the deposits in accordance with the rules? Don't fret, we'll cover the return of tenants' deposits, including deductions and disputes later on.

## 5.2.5 Zero Deposits

And before we move on, it's worth noting a new arrangement that has come into play these last few years, which involves a zero deposit. Here, the tenant has the option to request a zero deposit, and instead pay a smaller non-refundable amount (usually one weeks' rent) to a scheme such as:

*https://www.zerodeposit.com/landlords/*

The scheme then provides the landlord with deposit assurance worth roughly six weeks' worth of rent (amounts from different providers vary) in the event they need to deduct monies at the end of the tenancy.

So, the landlord gets the same protection offered by a deposit, but the tenant only has to pay one weeks' worth of rent upfront—so, better for their cash flow. Sounds good, right?

Party pooper time. I don't like the concept. Not that I've ever used them, and probably never will as I opt out of these when I market my properties.

I can see advantages of the scheme, in that tenants can often struggle with cash flow when they move between properties as they are usually required to pay one months' rent upfront and a five-week deposit on the new property, and this will be before they receive the deposit back from their old place. So, they potentially need to fund 14 weeks of rent (five weeks + five weeks + four weeks).

But, as well as reducing my exposure to potential unpaid rent or property damage, a deposit is a good way to gauge the financial status of a tenant. I don't want to encourage tenants who don't have any more cash than one month of upfront rent payment. Harsh perhaps. But if they were to lose their jobs or fall on harder times, I'd be the one paying for it. I'm running a business, so I need to protect myself.

Perhaps more controversially, I'd question their financial decision making if they chose to incur a one week rent cost (which they will never get back) instead of holding money in a secure scheme that they will get back as long as they respect the property.

Your decision, but just to make you aware of the option. Whatever you do, when it comes to tenants' deposits, make sure you follow the rules!

Time to bust a myth…

Myth: "I don't know how to collect and register a tenants' deposit."

BUSTED!

Although important, the rules around how to collect and register a tenants' deposit are really not that complicated, are they? And the practical process itself is even easier when using an online agent. They do it for you!

You can now confidently navigate this part of being a self-managing landlord.

## 5.3 Legal Obligations of a Landlord

It's not just having a tenancy agreement in place and ensuring you register tenants' deposits correctly. Oh no, if only landlord life was that simple.

There are now a VAST number of additional rules and regulations you have to comply with as a landlord. Daunting? Yes. Insurmountable? No way!

Yes, these must be done. But they are not complicated, so read the high-level summary of each of the rules below, and for each one, find out how you can easily comply with these at the click of a button. This book is designed to make life simple for landlords.

### 5.3.1 Energy Performance Certificate ("EPC")

This is an easy, yet essential one...

It is a legal requirement to provide tenants a copy of your property's Energy Performance Certificate (or "EPC") when you advertise the property.

An EPC shows a rating of a property's energy efficiency. They're primarily used by would-be buyers or renters to quickly see how much their energy bills will cost in their new house or flat.

The EPC is issued by an EPC assessor who will carry out a brief survey of your home before producing the EPC. The house is then placed on a colour-coded scale from A to G, with A being the most efficient with the cheapest fuel bills.

Your house's EPC rating will depend on:

- The amount of energy used per $m^2$.
- The level of carbon dioxide emissions (given in tonnes per year).

Properties with lowest ratings, F and G, cannot be let, so landlords have to invest in energy efficiency improvements—although there are some exemptions to this. Once issued, the EPC will be valid for 10 years.

How can you obtain one of these important documents, I hear you ask? Very easily is the answer.

You can, of course, use google to find an EPC assessor near your property.

*"Or you reduce your effort levels to even less clicks of the mouse, and use your online agent to order one. Makeurmove charge £69 for a certificate. That' s £6.90 per year over the 10-year life they are valid for. Bargain!"*

Once obtained, you can upload this to your property profile on their website and it will automatically appear when you advertise your property, thus fulfilling your legal obligations.

If you order a new EPC mid-tenancy, just send the updated certificate to your tenants.

Quick. Easy. Cheap. Order your EPC today.

### 5.3.2 Electrical Installation Condition Report (EICR)

Here's a new(ish) property regulation for you…

Since July 2020, for all new and renewed tenancies, there is a legal requirement for an electrical installation condition report ("EICR") to be in place. From the 1st of April 2021, this will apply to all tenancies.

All electrical installations deteriorate with age and use and should be inspected and tested at regular intervals to check whether or not they are safe for continued use. Faulty and old wiring is one of the main causes of electrical fires in homes. If a fire were to occur and the property did not have a valid electrical certificate, the insurance policy is likely to be invalidated.

Electrical inspection reports should be carried out by fully qualified, accredited, registered electricians. They will check the condition of the electrics against the UK standard for the safety of electrical installations, BS 7671 – Requirements for Electrical Installations (IEE Wiring Regulations).

*"Initially, I tried to find an electrician myself using google, but after being let down a few times, I used Openrent, who had one to my flat*

*in three days, with the certificate emailed to me a few days after."*
*(Alex, overseas landlord)*

The EICR report will detail any observed damage, deterioration, defects, dangerous conditions and any non-compliances with the current standard. If any dangerous or potentially dangerous conditions are discovered, the overall condition of the electrical installation will be declared to be 'unsatisfactory', and an advisory note added to the report detailing what remedial works are required without delay in order to remove the risk to those in the premises.

EICRs are valid for five years. Order yours in a few clicks on Openrent from as little as £159 (+£10 for every extra bedroom).

Ensure a copy of the EICR is provided to new tenants before they move in. You'll also need to send tenants a new certificate if you renew the EICR mid-tenancy. Obviously.

This is a new and slightly more expensive regulation to follow, but let's face it, making sure the property is electrically safe and sound is very important, so best get it done.

### 5.3.3 Gas Safety (CP12) Certificate

Does your property have gas? If no, skip this section. If yes, it's important to read on.

> Key rule: UK landlords with gas appliances and fittings, including central heating, boilers and flues, must conduct an annual safety check conducted by a Gas Safe registered engineer. Annual means every year.

Your legal duties as a landlord cover any gas appliances that you own and provide for the use of the tenants of your property.

Landlords must keep a record of the safety check for two years and supply new tenants with a copy of the certificate before they move in and within 28 days of completing a new check.

It is perfectly acceptable to keep the records of your gas inspection electronically, and many landlords find it far more convenient.

As long as you can produce a hard copy when needed (such as when new tenants are moving in), you keep it safe (i.e. you don't delete it from your electronic records) and it uniquely identifies the engineer (e.g. with a signature), having only an electronic copy is absolutely fine.

It's worth noting the distinction between gas safety checks (where you get the certificate) and the related servicing and maintenance activities that may need to be undertaken. As a landlord, you have the responsibility of ensuring all appliances (specifically boilers), as well as pipes and flues, are operating safely at all times.

The general recommendation is that maintenance is performed every 12 months to ensure proper functioning of the appliances.

How do you get one of these certificates? Same answer as always:

*"Book it through your online agent. It's a few clicks of a button, a two-minute job. As an example, Openrent charge £45 for the certificate, so certainly not an expensive purchase. Get on it."*

Final useful pointer when it comes to gas is that it's always a good idea to ensure your tenants know where and how to turn the gas off and what to do in the event of a gas emergency.

### 5.3.4 Furniture and Furnishings

This one sounds scarier than it really is…

The safety regulations apply to the following furniture provided in a rental property:

- Armchairs, three-piece suites, sofas, sofa beds, futons and other convertible furniture.
- Beds, bed bases and headboards, mattresses, divans and pillows.
- Nursery furniture and loose, stretch and fitted covers for furniture, scatter cushions, seat pads and pillows.

The furniture items excluded from the regulations are:

- Antique furniture (manufactured before 1950).
- Bed clothes and duvets.
- Loose mattress covers.
- Pillowcases and sleeping bags.
- Curtains and carpets.

For furniture in a rental property to comply with the regulations, they must carry a manufacturer's label, which must be permanent and non-detachable.

The reality is, for most landlords, these regulations are not an issue because they let their property unfurnished or part furnished.

> All furniture and furnishings in a rental property must comply with the 1993 amendments to the Furniture and Furnishings (Fire) (Safety) Regulations 1988.

*"For landlords wanting to furnish a rental property, my advice is to furnish with new furniture. Given that it is an offence to sell non-complying items, anything purchased new should be fine."*

Keep your proof of purchase and any other related documentation as future proof.

If you do decide to use second-hand furniture, then be very careful. Ensure that the correct labels are in place identifying the fact that the materials are fire-resistant.

Spend a bit of time going around your property checking for labels for existing furniture and you'll be fine. New items will have this label automatically.

As I said at the start, this property regulation sounds scary, but in reality, using common sense will ensure you comply once you have an awareness of the rules.

### 5.3.5 General Data Protection Regulation (GDPR)

Warning: you will probably need to drink a strong coffee before you read this section. I'd go for a double espresso.

So, in simple terms, GDPR is a new set of rules designed to give people more control over their personal data. Which seems fair. There's a lot more to the full legislation, I promise you. But let's keep it simple.

Does it apply to us lovely landlords'?

Well, yes, unfortunately it does. Because landlords typically use and store their tenants' personal information (e.g. name, email address, phone number, etc.).

*"In terms of complying with GDPR, this means, as landlords, we need to process and control our tenants' information in a transparent fashion."*

This includes explaining:

- What personal information we collect.
- Why we need their personal information.
- How we might use their personal information (including who the information might be shared with).
- How long their personal information is retained for.

So, what does this mean in practical terms? It means we have two actions:

1) Register with the Information Commissioner's Office. It costs £35-£40 per year to register. You can register here:

https://ico.org.uk/for-organisations/data-protection-fee/

2) Use Privacy Policies where personal information is collected.

All the documents/forms used by agents/landlords that gather personal information from tenants should contain a privacy policy, clearly explaining why, how and for how long their information is controlled and processed. This doesn't need to be fancy. Just a few lines answering the above.

The good news is that landlords don't need consent to process personal information, as long as the information will be processed under 'legal requirement', 'contract', 'vital interest 'or 'legitimate interests', which pretty much covers the reasons for why landlords would process information while managing a tenancy.

Now I won't name names here, but nearly all (except two!) the landlords I spoke with said they don't do step 1 or 2 from above, but if you are feeling like being a perfect landlord, register with ICO and ensure your documents have a privacy policy. Annoying but not too tough, hey?

### 5.3.6 Legionella Assessment

Let's get technical for a second. Put on your science hat. You know you want to.

Legionella is hazardous bacteria that can be found in water. In a residential property, Legionella can grow in water stored at temperatures between 20°C and 45°C degrees. If ingested or inhaled, water containing Legionella will lead to Legionnaires' disease—an infectious and sometimes fatal form of pneumonia. Sounds scary, right?

The risk of Legionella is particularly low in properties with combi boilers as the system keeps the water moving, giving the bacteria little chance to develop.

However, homes with open water tanks (usually older buildings) have a substantially higher risk of Legionella, as the water is more likely to be left to stagnate.

Landlords are not legally required to conduct a professional assessment or produce a formal certificate. Frankly, there is enough regulation ensuring homes are fit for purpose without this specific water quality regulation.

However, landlords do have a more general legal duty of care to protect the health and safety of their tenants—a part of which is to ensure their property's water is safe to drink and use.

To do this, landlords "can" carry out a Legionella risk assessment.

For rental properties with water systems that could pose a potential Legionella risk, it is recommended that a Legionella risk assessment is carried out once every two years, or before a new tenancy begins.

It's also a good idea to perform a risk assessment if there are significant changes to the property's water systems. These can be booked fairly easily and cheaply online.

*"Regarding Legionella, here's the main point: Most landlords won' t have any reason to suspect any issues with the water supply, so don't need to take any action at all."*

Don't let this scary-sounding rule worry you. Good old common sense in ensuring your property is habitable will ensure you are compliant here.

### 5.3.7 Portable Appliance Testing (PAT)

This is not a legal obligation for a landlord. But something worth being aware of and doing every once in a while…

Portable Appliance Testing ("PAT") is the checking of the safety of portable (as opposed to fixed) electrical appliances in your property. Confusingly, portable appliances include stationary equipment like fridges and washing machines, as well as things like TVs, kettles and space heaters.

Getting these appliances tested with a PAT is a great way to ensure and prove their safety, allowing you to efficiently fulfil your duties as a landlord.

From a practical point of view, different appliances need testing in accordance with their risk of breaking. High-use, highly portable appliances like toasters are far more likely to be damaged in everyday use than a stationary washing machine, meaning a landlord might responsibly have the former tested every two years, but the latter every four years.

*"Openrent charge £69 for this testing, which covers up to 10 electrical appliances."*

The Openrent price includes free plug and fuse replacements, with minor faults being corrected and the appliance retested. All, of course, done by an engineer compliant to carry out work in accordance with UK law. You'll get given a digitally accessible certificate of electrical safety.

Worth doing, right?

### 5.3.8 Smoke and Carbon Monoxide Alarms

This is really important to ensure your tenant is safe in your property.

Landlords are required to have at least one smoke alarm installed on every storey of their properties and a carbon monoxide alarm in any room containing a solid fuel burning appliance (e.g. a coal fire, wood burning stove, gas boiler).

The landlord is responsible for making sure the alarms are in working order at the start of each new tenancy. After the landlord's test on the first day of the tenancy, tenants should take responsibility for their own safety and test all alarms regularly to make sure they are in working order.

It is recommended that you instruct your tenants to test the alarms monthly and ensure that you can prove that they were in working order the day their tenancy commenced.

*"I always ensure my inventory clerk tests the smoke and carbon monoxide alarms and then records this in their inventory check-in report, which I have signed by the tenant."*

### 5.3.9 Homes (Fitness for Human Habitation) Act 2018

The act applies to the social and private rented sectors and makes it clear that landlords must ensure that their property, including any common parts of the building, is fit for human habitation at the beginning of the tenancy and throughout.

The list below sets out the factors that are considered when determining this:

- Repair
- Stability
- Freedom from damp
- Internal arrangement
- Natural lighting
- Ventilation
- Water supply
- Drainage and sanitary conveniences
- Facilities for preparation and cooking of food and for the disposal of wastewater

Use your common sense here. Would you be able and willing to live in your rental property happily? If so, you will satisfy this obligation.

### 5.3.10 Repairs & Maintenance

Under section 11 of the Landlord and Tenant Act 1985, landlords are responsible for keeping the following aspects of the property in good repair:

- The structure and exterior of the property.
- The supply of water, gas, electricity and sanitation (including basins, sinks, baths and sanitary conveniences).

- The installations within the property for space heating and heating water.

It's a grey and subjective rule. Keep your property well maintained with the rule of thumb, "Would I be able and happy to live here?" and you'll be fine.

### 5.3.11 How to Rent Checklist

Are you getting bored yet? Tempted to skip to the next chapter? Don't! This next one is key, and oh so easy.

Landlords should provide their tenants with a copy of the "How to Rent: The Checklist for Renting in England" when they start renting from you (either hard copy or email).

There is no legal requirement to provide this, however, landlords cannot use the section 21 (no fault) eviction procedure unless an up-to-date version of this guide has been provided to the tenant. When you get to the evictions section later in this book, you'll see how important this is.

This information is frequently updated, so search on GOV.UK for 'How to Rent' to ensure you have the latest version. It's free to download.

Sending this document to your tenants before they move in is essential.

*"Most online agents will automatically send this document to the tenants by email. To be doubly sure, I email them a copy myself and request they confirm receipt of the document."*

### 5.3.12 Disability

As landlords, we want to ensure that we are giving equal opportunities to all prospective tenants, and this includes making sure we comply with rules surrounding those with disabilities.

A disability is broadly described as any mental or physical impediment which impacts someone's day to day abilities. The impact needs to be long-term (greater than one year).

If this applies, then landlords need to make "reasonable adjustments" to their rental properties if this is requested by a tenant, unless there are "reasonable grounds" for refusing. Very grey, and I fully appreciate that the likelihood of these situations arising are small, but I just wanted to make sure you are aware of it. Do your best to be accommodating.

### 5.3.13 Right to Rent

I find this rule quite annoying. Landlords are UK business owners. Our mandate should not extend to UK immigration services by ensuring tenants are legally allowed to live in the UK. But it's a rule, and although we may not like it, we do need to adhere to it. Penalties for non-compliance are nasty. Take a breather before you read this next part...

Scarily, you could be sent to prison for five years or get an unlimited fine for renting property in England to someone who you knew or had 'reasonable cause to believe' did not have the right to rent in the UK.

This includes if you had any reason to believe that:

- They did not have leave (permission) to enter or stay in the UK.
- Their leave had expired.

- Their papers were incorrect or false.

You can also be fined if both of the following apply:

- You rent your property to someone who is not allowed to stay in the UK.
- You cannot show that you checked their right to rent.

As scary as that sounds, the possibility of imprisonment or a fine is extremely low. And can be avoided altogether by following these easy steps below:

On day of check-in, I remind tenants that they will need to bring photo ID (passport, visa, national ID card, driving licence) before I hand over the keys. Whilst not a government immigration official, I do my best to check the validity of the document (does it look authentic, in reasonable condition, photo matches their looks, name matches the tenancy agreement/references, not expired).

I then take a photo of this and, on the same day, email this to myself with the following text:

*"TENANT NAME checked into PROPERTY ADDRESS today as tenants on an AST for a fixed-term of X months.*

*My legal obligation as a landlord involves checking they have a right to rent, by seeing their Passport/Identity Card. These appeared valid, in good condition and have adequate time remaining until expiry. To the best of my understanding, I believe they have a right to rent.*

*I took copies of their documents, which I am recording in this email."*

It really is that simple. It's a best efforts basis, so make sure you do just that.

In case you are interested, the government guidance for this process is here:

*https://assets.publishing.service.gov.uk/government/uploads/system/uploads/attachment_data/file/573057/6_1193_HO_NH_Right-to-Rent-Guidance.pdf*

And I'm afraid to say it doesn't end there. As a result of Brexit, from 1st July 2021, landlords now also need to check that tenants from the EU, EEA or Switzerland have a right to rent in the UK.

This can be done in the same way as mentioned before by doing a physical check of their identification, but it can also be done using a Home Office online checking service: *gov.uk/view-right-to-rent*.

It's interesting to note that this latest Brexit related rule applicable to landlords changed during the writing of this book—a very good example of how fast rules can change. Which may sound scary. In fact, it's one of the myths: how can I keep up to date with the ever-changing legal requirements?

But it's an even better example of how, by making sure I have set up the right network of contacts and information sources, I can easily and quickly be informed about these changes.

This particular rule change I read about in the monthly magazine I subscribe to, received two different emails summarising the changes and have seen many Facebook posts on it. I couldn't possibly miss it! I'll be covering how you can set these up in the "getting help" section later.

### 5.3.14 Making Sure You Have the Right Permissions

If only life was so simple that you could make a decision to rent out your property overnight. Nope. There are multiple stakeholders who need to ensure you have at the bare minimum notified, and in most cases, obtained their permission to carry out your business of renting out your property.

You won't be the first landlord who is tempted to skip these approvals. In most cases, you probably won't ever get found out. Probably. But that's not a risk worth taking when approvals are usually fairly straightforward.

Yes, they do take time to obtain, and by notifying the relevant parties, there is a risk—albeit small—that they will say "no" or charge you a high fee for the privilege of providing their approval.

But not having these approvals is likely to open you up to penalties and will almost certainly invalidate your insurance—something that could easily come back to bite you! So, best get it done.

Here are some of the common ones:

**Lender:** Landlords usually require a Buy to Let ("BTL") mortgage instead of a residential mortgage. Sometimes you can have a residential mortgage but obtain a "consent to let", either for free, a small fee or higher rate of interest.

You can usually find out your options from your lenders' website or by calling them. The switch is sometimes easy and free, but does often result in an admin charge to provide the consent.

**Freeholder:** Own a leasehold property (flat)? If so, before you rent your property, you will likely need the freeholder's approval. Usually granted quickly and easily, although expect to get charged an admin fee for the privilege. While these admin costs are sometimes covered in the lease, the majority of times they charge just as a way of easily making a little more money.

You can challenge this (if you can be bothered—the costs are not usually that much) by requesting details of where the charges are covered in your lease agreement.

*"On a seemingly random basis, one of my freeholders reaches out asking for a £48 fee as I am letting my property. I email them back, asking where in my lease agreement this charge is shown. I've never heard back!"*

**Managing agent:** Communal Freeholders or leaseholders will sometimes have a managing agent who looks after their property, for which they will pay a service charge. Seek approval from these agents (not to be confused with estate agents) prior to letting your property, and again, don't be surprised if them saying "yes" involves you giving them a fee!

**Local council licence:** There is no UK nationwide landlord licence scheme for residential single let properties. However, some local councils are launching selective and additional landlord licensing schemes.

Most of these seem to be London based, so hopefully not relevant to the majority of landlords. You can check your local council website as the rules vary from council to council. Use this link to find your local council:

*https://www.gov.uk/find-local-council*

The average cost of a landlord licence is roughly £500 for five years. So, nothing too scary cost-wise if you need to obtain one of these. What is scary is the "up to £30,000 per offence" fine that can be charged to those landlords who are found not to have a licence.

I'll be honest, I'm not a fan of this licence at all. And when an accountant says, "I'm not a fan," they mean something much ruder!

I do like the concept of a consistent UK nationwide landlord licensing scheme, where best practice is promoted and enforced for all landlords. Having just a few councils sneak in a "licence" fee is simply just a way to raise for council income at the expense of landlords. It's not consistent.

**House in Multiple Occupation ("HMO") licence:** Little bit of background before we cover this potential licence requirement.

This book is written for residential landlords of single let properties. By "single let", I mean a property that is let to one tenant. Confusingly, one tenant can be multiple people (i.e. a couple, a family or two friends). But importantly, it means that there is just one tenancy agreement, with the relevant persons named on it.

A <u>house in multiple occupation</u> (HMO) is a property rented' out by at least three people who are not from one 'household' (for example, a family) but share facilities like the bathroom and kitchen. It's sometimes called a 'house share' with individuals having their own individual tenancy agreements with the landlords.

There are a whole set of different rules for this type of property rental, which I won't go into detail in this book. If this is what you do, please research the rules carefully online to ensure you comply with them.

You should check your local council (remember the link I gave earlier?!) to see what licensing you require. Big trouble for those landlords who don't comply here, so please make sure you do, to avoid a telling off with extras.

Anyway, having read this section, you now know how to comply with all the legal requirements. Which means it's time to bust a myth...

Myth: "I'm worried about complying with all the legal requirements."

BUSTED!

Getting the legal aspects right is crucial for landlords. And with so many legal rules to adhere to, it's no wonder that landlords can feel worried and overwhelmed when they first start out.

But you now know the rules that apply to landlords. Which makes them less scary. Even better, you know that complying with these rules is cheap, easy and can be done quickly online. Don't let the legal aspects put you off of self-managing your property. You can do it.

## 5.4 Landlord Insurance

Another section, another admission: I've never liked insurance. Car insurance, travel insurance, life insurance, and of course, property insurance. It's a hassle to set up, more expensive than what you want it to be, and you are always nervous whether some obscure hidden T&C will prevent you from claiming when you really need to.

But...

In the property rental space, insurance is an important (and in my ranty opinion, essential) part of being a landlord.

For the simple reason that by owning a rental property, you own a valuable asset. So, you naturally have more to lose if something goes wrong. Fire, flood, theft, damage. You could lose multiple thousands of £££s. It's, therefore, common sense to protect the value of your asset as best as you can. Reduce that risk, baby! Landlord insurance is one such way of doing this.

Firstly, let's remind ourselves of a few simple yet important points:

1) Landlord insurance isn't a legal requirement. Although because buildings insurance is a requirement of most mortgage lenders and many leasehold agreements, you'll likely need to get insurance, even if you don't want to.

2) A conventional home insurance policy is usually not valid if you're renting out your property, so you're likely to need dedicated landlord insurance. Nice try.

3) Insurance is unrelated to the topic and purpose of this book—i.e. it doesn't matter if you use a high street agent or self-manage your rental property (go you!), insurance is something you'll have to consider and arrange regardless.

Here's where it gets a little complicated. You can't just say, "Thanks, Louis, makes sense, I'll go grab myself some landlord insurance." No, no, no.

There's different types of landlord insurance. You need to be aware of these so you can choose which ones you want to purchase. You also need to be aware of the level of coverage you are likely to need.

Because I'm a helpful guy, here's a summary I prepared earlier of the main types of landlord insurance cover, to save you having to google it:

### 5.4.1 Landlord Buildings Insurance

Landlord building insurance covers the cost of repairing or rebuilding your rental property if it's damaged by something like fire, flood or vandalism.

If you own a flat and the freeholder is responsible for buying the buildings insurance, you can choose to get cover for your fixtures and fittings instead.

*"With the exception of one, my properties are leasehold, so the building insurance is provided by the freeholder. I do, however, always ask for a copy of the insurance certificate so I easily have it to hand if ever needed."*

The amount of landlord building insurance you take out should be based on the rebuild value of your property. This amount is different from the market value. It's the cost of rebuilding your property from scratch, including labour and materials. If you're struggling to accurately estimate this, you can hire a surveyor to help.

### 5.4.2 Landlord Contents Insurance

You can add landlord contents insurance to your policy if you want to cover furniture, appliances and decorative items. Bear in mind that this will only cover your possessions. Your tenants need to take out their own contents insurance to cover anything that belongs to them.

Landlord contents insurance can pay for repair or replacement if your contents are stolen, or if they're damaged by something like fire or flood. If you also want to protect them in the case of accidental damage, you'll usually need to add accidental damage cover to your policy.

You should base the amount of landlord contents insurance you take out on the cost of replacing all of your contents. This includes the furniture and appliances that you provide to your tenants like the fridge, television and sofa.

It's important that you estimate these values as accurately as possible so that you're covered if you need to make a claim.

### 5.4.3 Landlord Liability Insurance

Landlord liability insurance is designed to protect you against compensation claims made by a tenant or visitor for injury or damage that's blamed on your property. For example, if someone tripped on a loose floor tile in your house and suffered a serious injury, your landlord liability insurance could cover the legal fees and compensation pay-out.

You'll see coverage here varies quite a bit, and likely in the range of £1-£5M.

*"While it's unlikely you'll ever need this type of cover, I sleep a lot easier at night knowing I have this type of insurance for my properties."*

### 5.4.4 Accidental Damage Insurance

Accidental damage insurance can pay to repair your building or replace your contents if an accident happens, like a red wine spillage on your carpet or a hole in the wall because DIY has gone wrong. We've all done it and seen it.

If you buy landlord buildings insurance, then you can add accidental damage cover for buildings, and if you buy landlord contents insurance, you can add accidental damage cover for contents. Simples.

### 5.4.5 Legal Expenses Insurance

Legal expenses insurance can cover legal action that you need to take in relation to your rental property, for example, to pursue unpaid rent or to evict your tenants.

### 5.4.6 Tenant Default Cover (Rental Protection)

Tenant default insurance can protect your rental income if your tenants don't pay their rent. This is not available for all tenants and most definitely impacted by COVID-19. Policy terms will vary quite a bit in terms of amount and conditions.

*"I've never opted for this type of insurance as I have always done thorough referencing as a way to check my tenants have the best chance of being able to pay me each month."*

### 5.4.7 Emergency Breakdown/Assistance Cover

One final type to mention. Something that may be particularly appealing to self-managing landlords. You can pay for emergency breakdown cover.

Imagine your biggest fear comes true and you receive a call at 2 am from your tenant saying water is flooding into your rental property.

Panic. And a lot of cost.

You can pay to have this type of cost covered by insurance. You can pay even more and have someone available who will fix these types of issues.

Which, as a self-managing landlord, sounds like a dream. Except it comes at a cost. A pretty hefty one at that.

For me, that cost is not something worth paying for as the amount of times these things happen is very infrequent. But for those seeking more peace of mind, it's definitely worth considering. Ask your provider what they can offer.

### 5.4.8 Where to Actually Get Landlords Insurance

After reading the summaries on the types of landlord insurance, are you crystal clear on exactly what you need?

I won't take offence if you say no! Even with a short overview on each type, it remains a tricky area. Perhaps the reason I don't like insurance is because I find it overly complicated. I just want to say to an insurance provider, "I want landlord insurance that covers me for what landlords generally need without paying a ridiculous fee for the privilege."

Yet whenever I request this, I always end up being forced to go into the detail and emerging without being 100% sure if I've set it up correctly. Fingers crossed, hey!

Anyway, most landlord insurance policies include at least buildings insurance and landlord liability insurance, so you'll probably be fine. You can then choose to add other landlord insurance covers to your policy, like landlord contents insurance, accidental damage and tenant default cover.

So, the big question: Where do I get my landlord insurance?

*"I use RentGuard, which is the NRLA insurance partner. The pricing has always been reasonable to me with a good service provided—responsive and helpful to my many silly questions."*

My properties are leasehold flats, which means buildings cover is provided by the freeholder, so focus has been on getting content insurance along with liability insurance.

I've also used Simply Business before and found them to be fine. Jump on a comparison site and see what deals you can get. Don't overthink it. Just get it sorted.

## 5.5 Chapter Summary

- The most common form of rental contract is an assured shorthold tenancy ("AST"). A good quality AST is usually provided by your online agent.
- It's important to register a tenants' deposit with one of the approved government schemes.
- There are many legal requirements of being a landlord, all of which can easily be complied.
- As a landlord, you need to check you have the right permissions to rent out your property.
- Landlord insurance is a great way to protect your investment and reduce your risk.

# 6.0 PREPARING THE PROPERTY FOR CHECK-IN

Prepare. Such an important word for a landlord. Having found a tenant and made sure you are on top of the legal aspects, it's more than worth spending some time ensuring you, and the property are ready for them to move in.

A little more time spent upfront can have a significant beneficial impact on the future relationship with your tenant.

The (hopefully small) vacant period before the new tenant moves in is the perfect time to get any refurbishments done, have the property cleaned and ensure you have the right sets of keys ready. Utilities ownership can be set up or transferred and an independent inventory should be booked. You can even prepare a "how to" guide for your property.

And then finally, on the move day itself, learn how to do this properly and efficiently. Start as you mean to go on.

This section is all about the small details. And it' s these small details that can often make the biggest difference to your landlord life further down the line.

*"When I first let my property out, I only had one set of keys. My (two) tenants on check-in day weren't best pleased. I've never made that mistake again." (Lucas, landlord)*

## 6.1 Refurbishment Works

Let's start with a question that's always on the minds of landlords: How much refurbishment work should I complete before a new tenant moves in?

There are two schools of thought here. One is that unless a tenant has specified upfront that a certain repair or enhancement should be done prior to them moving in (something you would have agreed to as part of initial negotiations), these can be left alone. Why spend money on something when you don't need to, right?

I've certainly adopted that approach before, and in some cases, where your property is snapped up fast, you may not even have time between tenants to consider refurbishment of any kind.

However, after many years of renting out property, I now prefer a second option:

*"I continuously make enhancements or refurbishment work to my properties in the void period between tenants."*

I do this regardless of whether this is paid for by previous tenants out of their deposits (more on deposit deductions later) or requested by the new tenants.

Let's consider timing first. In the void period, not having a tenant in the property makes it so much easier for you, or your handyman/builder to properly assess the state of your property, and pick up on any works required.

Lightbulbs gone? Mould around the kitchen sink? Stains on the carpet? Messy garden? Marks on the paintwork? I want to know what these repair works are, and then I want to get them fixed prior to the new tenants moving in.

I now do this every time between tenants, and find that it's quick, easy and cheap to have these small items made good.

And the powerful long-term benefit? Well, the property continues to stay in great condition for many years to come. "A stitch in time" and all that.

*"The property is my asset. It's my business and I want to keep it in the best condition possible."*

What's more, once I've made these touch-up enhancements to the property, I ensure they are captured in the inventory report I always have prepared prior to check-in. That way, the tenant benefits from moving into a property in fantastic condition, but then has the responsibility of ensuring this condition is maintained themselves, with their deposit at stake as an incentive.

It's a win-win for all and will save you significant sums of money over time by reducing the frequency of major and expensive renovation works.

As well as refurbishment work and repairs, the void period before tenants move in is a great time to think about the style of your property, including the decorating and furniture.

Have a think about whether you can make the property more appealing. Perhaps the lighting can be improved. Or walls or floors can be redone in a way to appeal to more tenants in your target demographic.

While it may be appealing to decorate the property in your own preferred style, or add in unique features, it's generally seen as the best idea to stick with neutral styles and colours so as to appeal to as many prospective tenants as possible. That bright red feature wall you love may not get the same reaction from tenants!

Likewise, when it comes to price range, don't go for the most expensive. But also, don't go for the cheapest, as these tend to break much faster. Keep things mid-range, durable and neutral. Sounds a little boring, I'll admit, but it's also a sensible business decision.

And don't be afraid to show the tenant all the enhancement or repair works you've done. You've made an extra effort to ensure they will move into their new home in the best condition possible, something you should feel proud of and can greatly help the long-term relationship you will have with these tenants.

Pro tip: Don't expect to be openly thanked by tenants for doing these repairs. Lots of tenants will be grateful and show their appreciation, which is nice to receive, but others will appear fairly indifferent. Don't take offence! Everyone is different. The main thing is you doing your best to provide tenants a well-maintained home for them to live in, which increases your chances of having a better long-term relationship with them.

### 6.1.1 How to Find a Good Tradesperson

Some landlords are experts when it comes to dealing with repairs or maintenance at their rental properties. If that's you, feel free to skip this section.

Others, like me, are not. In fact, I'm terrible at this sort of stuff. And it's those of us in this latter category who greatly fear any type of refurbishment or maintenance work at our properties.

But luckily, we live in the 21st century. One filled with technology and social media. Which means that finding a good tradesperson can be very quick and easy.

Most tradespeople are honest, competent and hard-working. But some aren't, and if you go with one of these, you are likely to pay a lot more, be a lot more stressed, and have work completed to a poor standard (if at all).

Here's how to find a good tradesperson:

- **Use personal recommendations:** Has one of your friends or family recently worked with a tradesperson for a similar type of work and said they were good? If you've seen the work yourself first-hand, snap them up.

- **Facebook recommendations:** Facebook does everything, and one thing it does particularly well is the groups where you can post a question in a relevant group like: "Anyone know a good plumber who can fix a leaky toilet?" Post a message like this in a local community group and you will almost certainly get multiple speedy recommendations. Do watch out for self-biased reviews though, i.e. "I'm good and can help you"!

- **Taskrabbit and/or other apps:** I'm sure you've seen adverts for these new types of business apps. Download on your phone and easily search for tradespeople in your area. For each tradesperson, they show their reviews, availability and skills.

*"I've used Taskrabbit multiple times and have found some fantastic tradespeople from the app, who I work with to this day." (Amanda, North London landlord)*

If you are tempted, why not use this link to get £10 off your first task:

*https://www.taskrabbit.co.uk/s/6o9w7/try?utm_source=trycode*

(Other apps do exist.)

- **Checkatrade/Rated People/TrustATrader/MyBuilder**: These are the main sites for tradespeople, where they become members by undergoing background checks and have independent reviews submitted.

*"I used Checkatrade recently to have some garden maintenance work and removal work done at one of my properties, and found it an easy and stress-free process."*

- **Online searches.** If all else fails, google it.

Using one or some of the above methods will sort you a number of good tradespeople options that you can meet and request a job quote from.

I'd always recommend meeting and getting quotes from at least three different tradespeople (unless the job is really small, in which case, that's probably not needed).

You want to choose the best tradesperson though, so how do you narrow it down? Try this:

- Ask for previous customer references and follow up on these.
- Ask what insurance they have.
- Ask if they are a member of a trades body.
- Get a detailed cost quote for the work in writing (you need to be detailed in what you are asking for, then check whether the quote includes materials).
- Ask how/when they want payment.
- How professional do they seem?
- What is their availability?

All pretty simple stuff. Despite being rubbish at any type of refurbishment or maintenance work, I've been able to use the above pointers to easily find high-quality specialists, quickly.

And finally, don't overthink this when it comes to making a decision. Expect a bit of trial and error here when you are starting out. If the tradesperson you go with does a poor job, just search for someone else.

Fancy bustin' a myth?

Myth: "I don't know how to find and/or work with good tradespeople."

BUSTED!

I'm rubbish at DIY. When I first started self-managing my properties, I had no good tradesperson contacts either.

Yet I managed just fine.

That's because with just a little online research, a bit of trial and error, and then some time spent building trusted relationships, I easily found myself a great network of local tradespeople who I continue to work with to this day. Which means that maintenance or refurbishment works take up very little of my own time.

This can be you too.

## 6.2 Booking an Inventory

To earn 100 points and proceed to the next section, please answer the following question:

**Question**: What is the best way to protect yourself against damage to your property, and protect your tenants from having deposits held unfairly?

Cue drum roll and suspenseful music. And the answer is…

**Answer**: Get an independent inventory prepared and signed by both the landlord and tenant at check-in, AND at check-out. Simples.

For those who haven't come across these before, an inventory is a document that documents the state of the property at a certain point in time. It's something that can be prepared by the landlord or by an independent inventory clerk.

They will cover each room within the property as well as external areas such as gardens, garages, etc. Each area will have its condition described, including cleanliness, state of repair (i.e. marks on walls) and furniture provided along with supporting photos. They will note what keys are provided and check meter readings for the incoming tenants.

Another key job they will cover, which I mentioned in the legal section, is testing the fire alarm and carbon monoxide alarms are working and ensuring this is documented. Very important.

First things first. Don't do this yourself. Yes, you could save yourself £100(ish) but a) you won't be as skilled as a professional clerk at quickly capturing all the key items of note in the property, and b) more importantly, it's harder to argue the report is "independent" if needed further down the line if you've done it yourself (obviously).

Guess what? You can order these inventory reports through your online agents' website in a few clicks of a button, and someone will reach out to arrange a suitable time/day to attend the property, and will have a report back to you a few days later for you and your tenant to sign.

> Pro tip: Get the inventory report done a few days before the tenant is due to check-in so that you have the completed report available on move-in day. This will allow you to provide a printed or electronic copy to the tenant for them to check and physically sign when they first move in.

I always get inventory reports done, and always ensure it is signed by both myself and the tenant, even if that is just acknowledgement over email that the report is received.

I have sometimes found scepticism from tenants that their new landlord may be trying to trick them somehow, so I am always happy to mention that they are the main beneficiary of the report—it's something that any self-respecting landlord should do.

*"I ensure tenants are aware that they can propose changes to the report. As a tenant myself, I have requested changes that I wanted captured in the report. I emailed these changes to the agent who confirmed receipt of the comments—no new report needed to be issued, the written audit trail is there on email instead."*

An inventory report is there for everyone's benefit. Responsibility is with landlord and tenant to ensure it is as accurate as possible, and believe me, it can save a huge amount of pain further down the line vs not having one.

And finally, I don't really need to remind you of this, but when the inventory clerk is booked, make sure you send them a reminder before and on the day itself—just to be on the safe side.

## 6.3 Don't Forget the Basics

So, you've carried out some repairs on your property and ensured you've got an inventory report prepared. Almost there. Just a few little extra bits to bring yourself up to A grade prep status.

### 6.3.1 Cleaning

Linked to the previous section on refurbishment work and inventories is my strong recommendation to get your property cleaned prior to your tenants moving in.

I would ideally recommend you have the property "professionally" cleaned but I appreciate just how subjective this is, and why the industry has moved away from that terminology.

To you, professional cleaning may mean paying a business £300 for them to do a "proper" clean of all areas with a full range of cleaning equipment (carpet steamers, deep oven clean, etc.). To someone else, it could mean paying someone who advertises locally at £10 an hour for a few hours of their time.

You may even choose to clean the property yourself.

*"I don't clean the property myself as I prefer to pay someone who I know will do the job better, and doing it myself is not time effective for me. My wife always says I don't clean properly anyway."*

Each to their own.

Whatever you choose, it will cost you time or money to have this done. And that's fine. Remember, the state of the property is captured by the inventory report, and must be vacated in the same condition. So, in the future, you will (should) have it cleaned by the tenants to the same standard.

It's another win-win situation for landlord and tenant. Cleaner property for the tenant (particularly important in the COVID-19 era we now live in), and a higher chance the property will be kept that way during the tenancy, which is what landlords like.

A professional clean is a great way to set a first impression on check-in day, to welcome a tenant to their new home, as well as giving a perfect demonstration of how you expect the property to be maintained during their stay.

### 6.3.2 Keys

How many front door keys do you have? What about the back or garage door, and any window keys? Do you require a fob to enter a communal area? Or a code to enter a car park? Any special meter or utility cupboard keys?

Keys have a habit of getting lost. So, first, make sure you write down exactly what keys you have, and where they are stored.

*"I keep a key inventory list on email, so I always have it to hand on my phone if needed." (Bex, Warwick landlord)*

Then, have a think about how many sets you have of each key. I always go with one set for each tenant, then two spare sets. My properties are leasehold flats, so usually one of these spares is kept with the onsite concierge, the other I keep. These are on a keyring, clearly marked with the property name, in a place I always keep keys (which I think is in a drawer somewhere).

Keys are not complicated. Just make sure you are organised on this front before the tenants move in.

### 6.3.3 Utilities

Sigh. This is one of the parts I find most annoying about managing properties. It's not a fun or exciting job taking meter readings or registering with utility suppliers for the void period between tenants. It's very tempting to bury your head in the sand for these types of jobs.

However, I have forced myself to get better at this process, to add systems to streamline the process to minimise the time I spend on this part of the job. I'd encourage you to do the same.

Again, it's not difficult:

*"Simply write down and store the key utility information for your property somewhere. At a minimum, gas, water, electricity, council tax contact details and references."*

You can go further, documenting where meters can be found (not always obvious!), and recording readings on check-in and check-out day. These readings should also be on your inventory reports, so not something you have to do if you use an inventory clerk.

This one-off extra effort makes a big long-term difference to your ease of life as a landlord as the same information can be recycled to each new set of tenants as part of a welcome email.

### 6.3.4 Preparing a Guide to Your Property

Following on from utilities, here is one tip that will save you countless hours as a landlord. Write down everything you know about the workings of your property. Make it as detailed as possible and add photos and diagrams to assist further. It doesn't have to be perfectly written, or formatted or presented. Just get stuff written down.

This can be given to tenants (with them being told to check this in the first instance if there are any questions), and also serves as a good reminder to you—particularly useful if you don't visit the property frequently or have a bad memory like me!

So, what to write down? I've added a few ideas at the end of this section, in no particular order. I'm sure you can think of more for your own property.

Property guide content:

- How does the washing machine work?
- How does the dishwasher work?
- Any alarm system and how it works + code
- Where is the water stopcock?
- How do keys work? (It sounds simple, but some have a certain way")
- How does the central heating work?
- How do radiators work?
- Bathroom fan workings
- How does the oven/hob work?
- Instructions for any electrical devices (TV, etc.)
- Car parking details
- Bike storage (if any)
- Refuse collection details
- Utility cupboard/meters
- Power switches, including electricity fuses
- Concierge or caretaker contact details
- Resident groups' contact details (Facebook groups)
- Utility supplier details
- Phone number of local tradespeople (if you want)

Preparing this will take a few hours to produce, and again, isn't an exciting job. But having one of these documents will save you so many more hours over the years, it really is worth it.

Finally, remember that you are bound to forget things when you first produce this. The main thing is to remember to add to this whenever you find out something new, i.e. if a tenant asks a question you don't initially know the answer to, but eventually find out, write it down here.

### 6.3.5 Contact Details/Process

It's 9 pm on a Sunday night and water is pouring into your property from the flat above. Who does the tenant contact?

The tenant has noticed one of the radiators is not working. Who do they contact? And how?

Don't leave it to chance. Let the tenant know when and how they should contact you, and when they need to speak directly to someone else. Having a clear process works best for everyone.

For me, this is simple. I let the tenant know they can contact me any day/time they want via text, WhatsApp or email to report non-urgent items. I say that I check all of these fairly frequently, and "generally" expect to reply within 24 hours. In reality, I reply much sooner, but want to maintain a life outside of being a landlord, hence not promising a super quick reply time. I've never had an issue with this.

Have a think about what works for you. Then let your tenant know in a concise and polite way. Simple.

Obviously, for anything urgent, they can call. Calls should only be done to report something important and urgent, unless they have been pre-arranged.

*"I say to tenants that in the unlikely event of an urgent emergency where I am not contactable (for example, major water leak at night where I don't keep my phone on), the tenant is permitted to contact*

*an emergency plumber to have the issue resolved—something that I'd pay for. I also provide them the contact details of a 24/7 plumber."*

Now, before you say it, I get it! The definition of "emergency" or "urgent" is subjective, and can be the cause of disputes (you don't want a tenant calling an emergency plumber themselves to have a tap dripping noise fixed, for example).

Whilst you have to hope that common sense prevails, letting tenants know your expectations upfront gives you the best chance of avoiding any tricky conversations down the line.

And finally, do you know any good local handymen or plumbers who know you and the property well, and who you trust (we covered finding people like these earlier)? Why not give the tenants their contacts details so they can contact them directly? Give clear instructions on what types of work and any cost limits that apply (give the same to your tradespeople) and cut your role as middleman down.

*"Nothing makes me happier than my tenants talking to my handymen/plumbers directly—efficiency maximisation!"*

So, how to tell tenants about this process? Again, easy—send them a short email summarising how it should work, including your phone number or email address or whatever contact method you choose to use. Then mention it to them again at check-in to ensure the message is taken on board. Job done.

Anyone else feel that it's time to bust a myth?

Myth: "I'm worried my tenant will call me at midnight on Sunday every week."

BUSTED!

As a landlord, it's inevitable we will get contacted occasionally at times we'd prefer not to be disturbed.

But these disturbances should be very infrequent. And only for serious items that genuinely warrant your attention.

For everything else, the tenant should be given a clear set of instructions on how and when they are expected to contact you, or someone else.

Don't leave it to chance and risk being disturbed unnecessarily. Be organised and you really don't need to worry about this as a landlord.

## 6.4 Getting it Right on the Day

Having worked through the above steps, on check-in day itself, you can feel pretty confident you have done everything possible to ensure a smooth check-in, in what is hopefully the start of a mutually beneficial long-term benefit to both parties.

It's exciting. Your new tenant moves in today. There's a few final points to remember to ensure you've given your tenant, and you, the perfect start to this tenancy on the day.

But first, let's be clear. Before the tenant moves in, you need to have received your first months' rent upfront, as well as their deposit. Not pending a bank transfer or a logistical setback. If, for whatever imaginative or logistical reason that rent is not in your bank account (or the online agent confirms they hold the funds), DO NOT HAND OVER THE KEYS.

I've never had this happen to me, but I know it can happen. Even though it's unlikely, given the legal contract you now have in place, along with the robust referencing you have applied, these things can happen.

> On check-in day, the rule is simple: No rent received upfront, no keys.

And any attempt to delay paying rent, or excuses as to why it's slightly late (unless the tenancy has genuinely been agreed by both parties last minute, which is valid), is a big red flag.

But let's not dwell on the negative, and also highly unlikely eventualities.

Today is a day of positivity. You are about to start a new tenancy, and give your new tenants the keys to their new home. You have the ability to manage this like a pro, and give everyone the perfect start to the new relationship.

First, remember that pro-active communication with the prospective tenants during the viewings process? Well, now it's time to apply those skills again.

Don't be afraid to be in regular contact in the weeks and days leading up to the move-in date. Make sure it's clear exactly when and where you will be meeting them, and most definitely include a reminder before you travel.

Worst thing you can do on the day? Get there late! Whatever time you've agreed with your tenant, make sure you get there with plenty of time to spare. Give yourself some buffer for traffic, train delays, etc. It gives you time to do a final check on the state of the property, along with turning on lights, opening windows, even a light spray of air freshener to give the best impression.

How do I like to welcome my new tenants to their new home? With a small gift, of course! Not all landlords would agree with this. Some would argue this is a business relationship, and it's better to keep it strictly professional. I.e. the minute you start to become "friends" is when things are more likely to go wrong. Each to their own on their personal landlord style.

*"To me, giving the tenant a small gift when they check-in is one of those small details that can make a huge difference to the long-term relationship you are about to embark on."*

Wine, chocolates, flowers. Whatever you feel most appropriate. It doesn't cost much but has always brought a warm smile to my new tenants' faces.

Once you've done your warm greetings, walk the tenants through the property and surrounds, i.e. garden, communal areas or access ways. Show them as much as you can, without overstaying your welcome (remember, it's their home now!).

It's so much easier to show them how things work when you are there in person, rather than getting multiple messages for the next few weeks.

Items like what keys they have and how to operate (not all keys are simple!). Where is the water stopcock? How does the washing machine work? Heating. TV points. Utility meters. You don't need to spend hours describing these in detail, but a quick overview is beneficial to everyone.

Being a pro landlord means you will have a guide to your property (I know you've already done this—well done), which you can print out for them, along with your contact details and any other relevant information.

And finally, remember those right to rent checks covered in the legal chapter? Well, don't forget to see your tenants' ID (yes, you will probably need to remind them on the day to bring it!), then make a written record of you seeing this like I described in the legal section.

And then? Leave them to it. It's now their home.

Open up a good bottle of wine.

## 6.6 Chapter Summary

- Finding good tradespeople is a relatively simple process.
- Always get an independent inventory clerk to perform an inventory check-in report which is signed by both you and the tenant.
- Before a tenant moves in, make sure you have enough keys, have the property cleaned, and transfer over any utility bills.
- Preparing a guide to your property for your tenants can make your landlord life so much easier.
- Check-in day is the perfect time to start the new landlord/tenant relationship off on the right foot.

# 7.0 ONGOING PROPERTY MANAGEMENT

Maintain. Having taken the time and care to set up and prepare for the new tenancy, it seems only right that you would want to maintain that high level of professionalism throughout the tenancy.

To do that, you need to adopt a professional business mindset.

Having this mindset will make you a happier landlord, I guarantee it. Your relationship with stress and worry will change for the better once you understand the meaning of "controlled worry". You deserve a good nights' sleep.

This business mindset will also help you maintain and prosper from a mutually beneficial long-term landlord/tenant relationship. Your tenant is your customer. Treat them with respect, provide them with a high level of service, and you will reap the rewards. You both will.

As part of adopting this business mindset, you'll learn how to implement business systems that save hours of your precious time. Don't be a slave to your business, systemise it instead. This chapter will show you how to easily implement the best systems. And it's simple stuff really. Think rent collection, renewals, storing contacts efficiently and using a good old-fashioned diary.

*"Anyone can follow the steps in the previous chapters and become a self-managing landlord. But to do it the right way, to be the best landlord you can be, you need this chapter!"*

## 7.1 Having a "Business" Mindset

Life as a landlord. It all starts with mindset, and getting this right. Let's break it down.

Remember a rental property is not just a property. It's an investment, something you purchase to make money from. In fact, as a landlord, your property is even more than just an investment. It's a business, regardless of how many properties you rent out.

> A business is defined as an organisation where people work together. In a business, people work to make and sell products or services. A business can earn a profit for the products and services it offers.

Reading through that description, it's easy to see why your rental property should be treated as a business:

- It requires people (you and other stakeholders) to work together, be it with tenants, mortgage lenders, cleaners or tradespeople.
- You sell a service (a home for a tenant to live in).
- You (hopefully) earn a profit for the service you offer (be that recurring income or future capital gain—or both).

I'd also add that owning and renting out a property involves making strategic decisions, dealing with cash flows and requires time input from you as the landlord—all things, along with many others that I'd associate with a running a business.

As such, your rental property should be given the same time, respect and mindset as if you were running a business.

Having this business mindset is key if you want your property business to perform well.

There are three main areas within a business mindset that are crucial to the success of your ongoing rental property management:

1) "Controlled worry": Understanding and adopting this mindset will help you manage stress and reduce worry. You'll be happier!

1) Build mutually beneficial long-term relationships with tenants by treating them as business customers.

2) Put appropriate business systems in place to ensure you run an efficient business, reducing the time you spend managing property.

Let's take a look at each of these in detail.

### 7.1.1 "Controlled Worry" – How to Reduce Stress and Worry

*"Confession: As a landlord, I regularly feel scared. Wow. It feels better to write that down. Is that normal? Is that acceptable?"*

The answer is "Yes" to both of those questions, although with a caveat for the second question.

It's perfectly normal for landlords to worry, or feel scared, or stressed. There's 1001 different reasons why landlords might feel this way.

After all, we own an expensive asset (a property) and expect to receive monthly income (rent) from that asset. That means we have more to lose.

A property business also has bills to pay, decisions to make, risks to manage, customers (tenants) and other stakeholders (lenders, suppliers, etc.) to keep happy.

Each of those tasks bring risk. Which quite rightly brings worry (and the feeling of being scared). And often stress.

That is perfectly normal. Don't shy away from that. You run a business. Things can go wrong. It would be worrying if you didn't worry about it! It's a natural human emotion.

But how much worry is acceptable?

Here's my caveat (gosh, I love that word). While feeling scared is perfectly normal as a landlord, there's a limit to how much worry you should have. You can't spend your whole life worrying.

Instead, you need to adopt a mindset I call "controlled worry".

**Controlled worry**: Only worry about things that are within your control.

If something is outside your control, you simply shouldn't worry about it. If the source of worry is within your control, think about what next best action you can take to mitigate the risk, and therefore, the worry.

Keep prioritising the actions within your control until there are no additional actions within your control that you can take. It's only then you can't, and therefore, shouldn't worry. Use any worry you feel during this process to motivate you to focus on just the next best action you can take.

Let's use some practical examples for this:

*"I'm worried my tenant may not pay me rent."*

They may pay you the rent. They may not pay you the rent. You don't know, and won't until the day itself when the rent is due and the cash either will or won't land in your bank account.

Think about what you can control in the process. You can reference the tenant before entering into the tenancy agreement. This will show you whether they can afford to pay the rent or have ever defaulted or been late to pay before. You can also send the tenant a reminder about payment on the day. If you've done all that, why worry?

Let's say the unlikely event happens and the payment doesn't hit your account. Then, and only then is it reasonable to worry. But only a little, as you simply work out what your next best action is.

In this example, you'd contact them to remind them. Depending on whether you get a reply, you'd either be fine (paid) or need to chase or consider alternative actions.

Whatever actually happens, the process remains the same: You action the next step, get the result, and decide on the best action.

Worry can be there, but never as a controlling emotion. You control the worry and focus on items within your control that can eliminate the worry.

Let's try another example:

*"I'm worried that something might get damaged in my property that would be costly to repair."*

Things can go wrong at your property at any point, either by accident, or by misuse. At some point in your life as a landlord, this will almost definitely happen.

How can you reduce this risk? Make sure you get good landlord insurance to cover you for the bigger items. You can reference tenants to filter out those more likely to damage a property, and make regular checks and inspections of your property, so you can spot and resolve any issues early doors. You could even maintain a cash buffer in a separate bank account so you have funds available in case of unexpected costs.

If you haven't done all those steps, there is some justification to your worry. Controlled worry only though, as you'll use that worry to motivate you to prioritise doing the next best action within your control. Once you've taken all those actions, there is no justification to worrying. You've done everything within your control and can sleep easy.

There are so many more examples I could list, but you get the point. It comes down to having a "controlled worry" mindset. Adopt this mindset and you can sleep easy (easier at least) at night knowing you have done everything possible to reduce risks associated with your property.

But...

Even with the best processes in place, you need to accept that things will always go wrong at some point. That's unavoidable. There's no point worrying over something outside of your control or that you can't predict. That part is not healthy or acceptable worry.

So, to conclude, if you find yourself feeling scared, ask yourself: Have I put in place processes to manage this risk to as minimal level as possible?

- If the answer is yes, then don't worry. You've done everything you can. Go to sleep.
- If no, you are right to worry. Controlled worry only though. This worry is good and functional, which you can use to focus

your attention on an area within your control that requires improvement. Once all these are done, you can stop worrying.

### 7.1.2 The Landlord/Tenant Relationship

In this book, I've referred to the term "tenant" countless times. Because that is a term everyone instantly recognises, including your legal agreements.

What if I now told you to scrap that term?

Not because the term "tenant" is wrong or impolite in any way. It's simply because there is a better term to use:

Customer.

Say it. How does that sound? Customer.

You own and run a business. Who pays your income? Who do you need to keep happy? That's right, your tenant (sorry, I mean customer).

Now, let's be clear. I'm not asking you to redraft your legal agreements to replace "tenant" with "customer". Only to change your perception of your tenant to that of a business customer.

This simple mindset change will make a HUGE difference to the success of your rental property business. It will help you maintain and prosper from a mutually beneficial long-term landlord/tenant relationship.

One that plays out a bit like this…

You as the landlord provide a high-quality home to a customer, in exchange for a fair rent.

The customer will take good care of that property and pay the rent in full and on time.

You will ensure any issues within the property are quickly and properly addressed.

The customer will be happy with their home and want to stay there for a long period of time.

The landlord will be happy that their business is performing well financially, and does not require too much of their time.

Nor is it stressful when both parties of the business relationship are happy.

Win-win!

Ok, so not every landlord/tenant relationship works exactly like the above example, but this is the sweet spot you are aiming for. Start by referring to tenants as customers (just in your head) and notice the difference in how that feels, and how you treat the correspondence with your customer.

Now, before we go dancing off into the hills holding our customers' hands in blissful happiness, let's remember that we won't always be in the sweet spot.

There may be moments where you do have to be tougher and have awkward conversations. The tenant may not act in a reasonable manner and action may have to be taken, which you would prefer not to do.

These relationships will also likely involve compromise and effort from both parties to ensure their smooth running during the course of the tenancy.

And that's fine. That's business with its many ups and downs.

But at the back of your mind, you should always be thinking with a "customer" mindset, and working towards that sweet spot, whatever your current situation is.

Let's bust a myth…

Myth: "I can't deal with the stress of day to day management of my property."

BUSTED!

Can landlord life be stressful? Yes. Can you deal with it? Big thumbs up!

That's because you now have a few tricks (skills) up your sleeve that will help you deal with stressful situations.

With a "controlled worry" mindset, you won't be worrying about the multitude of things that could (but probably won't) go wrong. Instead, you'll focus on those items within your control where you can reduce risk and chances of stressful things happening.

Dealings with tenants will also be so much easier when you think of them as customers. Enjoy the relationship with them, including the day to day interactions.

Smile!

### 7.1.3 Implement Business Systems

Any successful business is built on a foundation of well-implemented systems. These allow the owner (landlord—YOU) to focus on the key strategic high-value items, saves you a huge amount of time, reduces your stress, and helps you comply with all the legal requirements. Systems are SO important, they are worthy of their own sub-chapter!

## 7.2 It's All About Systemisation, Baby

Want to be a happy landlord with plenty of spare time outside of managing your rental properties? Of course you do. Which means you NEED to implement systems to make sure your business (aka rental property) runs smoothly. More money, less time, less worry and happier. That's what this book is about.

> A word of warning: Fail to implement systems in your property business, and you'll waste hours of time running around putting out unnecessary fires. Ignore this section at your peril!

Here's the good news: Systems don't have to be complicated or require expertise to implement. In fact, the best ones are usually the simplest, as you'll see from my favourite systems I've implemented over the years. These make the ongoing property management so much easier to manage.

The great thing about advice on systems is that you pick those you like, and can enhance or tweak these according to your own situation, personality and preferences. And if you can think of other good ones not on this list, please do share.

Here's my top 10 systems:

### 7.2.1 Store Contacts and References Efficiently

How many times have you tried but failed to remember the phone number of a handyman? Or lost the email address of the solicitor you used four years ago? Or had to sift through countless drawers to find reference of your utility provider?

*"Losing key contacts and references used to happen to me a lot. And each time it was annoying, stressful, time-consuming and inefficient trying to go through old emails, documents or my memory to locate the contact details. No wonder I don't have much hair."*

Instead, how about if you have all your property contacts and references categorised and listed in one place? Imagine that, any time you need to remember/contact someone, you can go to that same place and find the phone number, email, address and even website for them immediately.

Life would be easier, right?

Here's the best bit. You don't need a fancy app, website or system to do this. Instead, you can use:

- The notes section of your phone/laptop.
- Your phone contacts and sync this with your laptop/other devices (this is what I do).
- Maintain a contacts and references document (Excel spreadsheet?).
- Use social media (Facebook, Google, etc.).
- You can even handwrite them down. Old school! But if that works for you, then go for it.

There's lots of other ways you can do this. You don't need training or fancy skills for any of these. Just a few hours for the initial setup and then ensure you a) keep a backup, and b) use consistently and maintain the list going forward.

Want to take it one step further like a pro? Why not:

- Add speed dial functionality for your key contacts. 1. calls the tenant, 2. calls the estate agent, etc.
- Add key references to contacts. No point having the number of the electricity company if you don't have their reference stored in the same place. Same for insurance and mortgage references.
- If you have multiple properties, categorise contacts according to each property.

So, if you are not already doing this, my advice is to think about a contacts storing process that would work best for you, then schedule in a few hours to set this up.

At the bare minimum, just promise me one thing: Any time you find yourself cursing that you can't find a property contact or reference, ask yourself, "How can I avoid this happening next time?" and then action that.

### 7.2.2 Rent Collection Process

It's highly likely the reason you are a landlord is your desire to gain financially from renting out your property. Which means receiving rent from your tenant is quite important.

And yet, it never ceases to amaze me how many landlords forget the rent collection part of property management.

*I've heard so many stories and read countless posts about landlords who, after six months of not checking their bank statements, suddenly realise they have not been paid any rent.*

These landlords then have to rush around in a panic to try and get things back in order. Collecting six months of backdated rent is not something I would look forward to.

Don't let that be you. Rent collection is such a simple part of being a landlord, and when set up correctly, is also stress-free. It doesn't matter if your online agent collects rent from the tenant directly and then pays you, or if you receive the rent directly from the tenant.

At some point in the month, likely based on the tenancy agreement start date, rent will be due. And guess what? A month later, on the same day, the rent will be due again. It's not difficult. It's not a moving target you have to constantly adjust for.

So, how to ensure it doesn't get forgotten? Set up a very simple yet effective system to remind yourself to check rent has actually been received. You use a paper diary (does anyone still use those?!), Google calendar, work calendar or have a personalised calendar on the fridge with pictures of your kids on it.

Whatever diary/calendar you use to manage your life and therefore should be checking frequently, mark in that EVERY MONTH for the next 12 months, or however long the tenancy lasts, when your rent should be received.

*"For my property bank account (Monzo), I get automated alerts on my phone whenever cash is received. Which means in nearly all cases, I see a "rent received" notification first thing in the morning. Just in case the rent doesn't come through, I have a reminder set on my phone."*

For the rest of the month, you no longer need to think about this. That is how to reduce stress as a landlord. The simplest and yet most effective system. Completely free to implement and maintain.

Now, there are some extra considerations worth noting:

Let's say your tenant pays your online agent, who, in turn, passes on that rent to you (this is how some of my properties operate). When you first set up with the online agent, check with them how long they take to process rent. Same day, next day, four working days, etc. These days, it should really be a same day transfer. Whatever processing date they confirm, mark your calendar with that date each month, and check your bank statements that day. Easy.

I'll cover non-payment in the next chapter, but something I also like to do is ask my online agents to notify me **the same day** if a tenant ' s rent has not been received on time. I don't want to wait for any investigation or admin delays on their side (not that I've ever had these). It's an easy way of keeping stress low. Unless I am notified, I do not need to worry.

*"Once, a tenant didn't pay my rent on time, and the high street agent I was with at the time only told me about it three weeks after it was due. I was furious!" (Paolo, landlord)*

Where tenants pay me directly, I encourage tenants to set up standing orders. In most cases of late rent payments, it's due to tenants forgetting, rather than it being a genuine issue. Standing orders automate the rent payments, reducing admin time for tenants and landlords.

I'll admit, I'm not perfect on the rent collection front. I can feel your shock and horror at reading this! But alas it's true. One of my tenants hasn't set up a standing order and has paid manually for the last 18 months (on time and in full, I should add) as that is her preference.

This meant that I was sending her text reminders each month when the rent was due. Not my preferred setup, yet it works fine, and is something I've managed to streamline as much as possible: I have a calendar reminder and a standard message I copy, paste and then send to her each month. Takes me less than two minutes to send, and rent is usually received within the hour of me sending.

It's something I deliberately highlight because I want to demonstrate how each landlord/tenant relationship will have something unique about it.

> The key point is that you and your tenant know when rent is due, and have reminders and systems in place to ensure that is followed.

And finally, for those with more than one property, why not take your rent collection to the next level? Something popular amongst pro landlords is structuring their rent collections so that they are all due on one day each month—usually the first of the month.

This does involve more work upfront as the initial rent payment will need to be pro-rated. For example, for a tenancy that starts on 14th April, the tenant will pay 17 days (14th April - 30th April) worth of rent in their first payment due on 14th April, and then a full month of rent for subsequent months, starting 1st May.

This has the benefit for those with multiple properties that you only need to check your bank account on one day each month, rather than multiple times. Have a think about whether that would work better for you.

Whatever you do, don't be the landlord who forgets to check rent is received. Put a simple process in place to ensure you get your rent, in full, on time, every month.

### 7.2.3 Visiting the Property

You own an asset (property) worth a fair bit of money. You've worked hard to ensure you are legally compliant and have a happy tenant paying rent and looking after your property. Sit back and relax? Well, yes, to some extent you can. But there' s no harm in checking your property is actually being well looked after.

The frequency of property visits depends on you, your tenant and the relationship you have with them.

Generally, at the start of a tenancy, you may wish to visit more frequently to double-check the tenants are looking after it. But once you've seen and are happy with the condition the first time, and have started to build a mutually trusting relationship, the frequency can be dropped.

This allows tenants more "quiet enjoyment" and reduces the time you need to spend on managing your properties. Even for longer and well-established relationships, I'd always recommend you visit the property once a year, usually before renewing the contract, just to be sure.

> For property visits, one important thing to note is that you are legally required to give your tenant at least 24 hours' notice of your intended visit, and visit the property at a reasonable time of day, unless it's an emergency and you require immediate access.

Some fairly subjective words there: "Reasonable" and "emergency". Everyone would define these differently. Use common sense, be fair to tenants and give them 24 hours' notice (3 am un-announced visits, not cool).

When there, these visits don't have to be long or detailed. Normally just a quick look into each room, ensuring no obvious issues (damp, mould, marks on flooring/walls, gardens maintained, etc.).

Remember, it's the tenants' home, so their style, cleanliness or level of clutter may be different to yours. That's fine. Don't judge. Really, you just want to make sure it is safe with no major damage. Get in and get out as soon as you can to leave them to enjoy their own home!

And finally, don't rely on your brain to remember when you should next view your property. Add a recurring reminder into your diary for your chosen frequency so you don't forget this important part of being a landlord.

### 7.2.4 Renewals

At some point, the fixed-term of the initial tenancy agreement will expire, so you will need to consider the renewals process. You'll know from the earlier legal section that you can move onto a periodic rolling tenancy, or enter into a new fixed-term agreement. Not renewing, thus ending a tenancy, is the other option—we'll cover that in the next chapter.

Let me put it out there:

*"I love renewals. They are the perfect sign of a good working business relationship for both parties, i.e. the landlord AND the tenant."*

And that's the best form of property rental: Happy tenants, a well looked after property and financially beneficial for the landlord.

Renewals save you a tonne of work and expense. Remember the earlier section on working out the cost of a void period? Well, a renewal keeps the same tenant in your property for another period of time, and in the process, guarantees you zero void as the new contract will commence as soon as the old one expires. Zero days of missed rental income. LOVE IT.

It also saves you the workload involved with advertising and letting a property out to new tenants. The time (and, therefore, cost) saving of this is big.

And for those reasons, I do my best to ensure tenants renew their contract when they are due (with the obvious caveat that I'd only do this if they are good tenants!).

So, assuming they are good tenants (i.e. pay rent on time and look after the property being my main conditions here), what do I mean when I say "do my best"?

Well, I simply make the renewal as appealing to the tenant as possible. Just as any business would offer when trying to keep an existing customer or win a new customer, I offer tenants nice things. It's not rocket science!

So, what's appealing?

*"Appealing could be offering to pay for a professional clean to spruce the place up, or sort some repairs/enhancements or provide additional furniture. I've even offered a slight reduction in the rent."*

A rent reduction might sound ludicrous but knowing the cost of a void, and the saving I make by a-void-ing (see what I've done there?!) this, means I can offer a small rent reduction in the knowledge that I stand to gain even more in the medium to long-term from this renewal. And in doing so, I've also got an even happier tenant. Win-win again.

Now it's worth noting that none of the above freebies are required. And in lots of cases, they may not be needed, i.e. if the tenant is proactively wanting to renew, this may just be a simple case of drafting a new agreement on the same terms. But I do want to highlight just how much you stand to gain from a renewal with a good tenant. You can make your own call on how best you can facilitate this.

In terms of practical steps, my key recommendation is to proactively reach out early to the new tenants. I usually first reach out a month or two before the final day of the current tenancy. I want the tenant to have plenty of time to consider their options, and also ensure we have enough time to negotiate and sort new legal documents if required.

*"I have a reminder in my calendar three months before my tenants' contract expires. I like to reach out to them as early as possible to allow plenty of time on all sides to get the renewal sorted." (David, Brighton landlord)*

Start with a simple message reminding them of when the fixed-term is due to expire. With good tenants, I then like to upfront say how much I've liked having them in the property, and how I'd be delighted if they would like to renew their contract [then insert details of any proposed changes to the terms of the contract if relevant]. And then ask them what their preferences are.

Sometimes you'll get a "no, thanks,", sometimes a "yes please, where do I sign?", and in most cases, a "yes, but [insert something tenant would like to negotiate on]".

From a legal perspective, you have two main options. Move onto the periodic rolling tenancy or renew for a new fixed-term. Most tenancy agreements will automatically move to periodic after the expiry of the fixed-term. I use both types of renewal. Periodic is easier and offers both parties more flexibility, but lots like to lock down a new fixed-term for peace of mind.

In terms of legal agreement and any specific clauses, similar considerations are needed to when you are first deciding whether to rent your property to the then prospective tenants.

However, this time, you have a bucket load more information about your tenants, which makes the decision so much easier. Renewals really shouldn't be stressful.

Key advantage of renewals: You don't need to speculate whether the tenant will be able to pay you the rent, or damage your property. They will have already lived there for at least six months, so you know that they pay rent and look after your property (because if they aren't doing those two things, then you of course won't be considering a renewal).

I'd say the biggest consideration is whether you want to push for a rent increase. Lots of landlords would say this is a must: Keep rents in line with inflation, keep increasing your income.

Only YOU will know what feels right for you based on how the tenancy has been for the first fixed-term. Just remember the cost of a void. Don't push too hard for a rent increase only to find yourself with an unnecessary and much costlier void.

So, let's talk practical considerations. If you opt for moving to a periodic tenancy, there is very little to do. Confirm this with your tenant that you are both happy with this and you are all done. No need to re-register a deposit, or issue any new legal documents. Simples.

Entering into a new fixed-term contract does require a new agreement. You can get this done quickly and easily via your online agent. The tenant's deposit will need to be re-registered and the prescribed information sent to the tenant. For completeness, I usually send the tenants an email with the following documents:

- The original tenancy agreement
- The renewal contract
- The deposit prescribed information
- The EPC/EICR/Gas certificate
- The original inventory
- The government how to rent guide

You can, of course, draft a renewal agreement or addendum to the original tenancy agreement yourself. Download one of the many examples online or get one from the NRLA. Personally, I find it easier to make use of the electronic signing options available from using your online agent though.

### 7.2.5 Repairs and Maintenance

As a landlord, it's impossible to avoid dealing with repairs and maintenance of your property. Things will break, require touching up, or need replacing. It's part of the job and fully expected. Your "controlled worry" mindset means you won't worry about what things could go wrong, just focus on what you can control when things do go wrong.

For a systemisation perspective (which is what these types of repairs really boil down to), there are some key points to note.

You know from the earlier section how to go about finding good tradespeople. As a starting point, make sure you have their contact details saved down in an easily accessible place.

Here's where you can make a difference to the long-term success of your business. If a contractor does a good job, at a good price, in a reasonable timeframe and is nice to deal with…

Pay them well, and pay them promptly.

Please re-read the above sentence.

Think back to the business mindset. If a business finds a good supplier, they treat them well. You need to adopt this mentality with your tradespeople.

Good payment terms are a good starting point. Clear communication and praise will further aid this.

Build that relationship. Work with them again. Keep growing it. Reach the sweet spot where you have a trusting relationship that you can ask them to liaise directly with tenants, and trust their judgement over what work is required and the costs involved.

*"It took me a while—at least a year—to reach with some trial and error along the way, but I have now reached this point. And it makes a huge difference."*

For any issues reported by tenants (assuming I don't have clarification questions to the tenants first), this is now my process:

- Reply to tenant:
    - Apologising for any inconvenience.
    - Informing them that I will get someone round ASAP.
    - Check if it's ok to give their contact details to the tradesperson (it always is).

- Message relevant local tradesperson:
    - Copy tenants' message with issue details.
    - Ask if they can investigate.
    - Provide tenants' contact details and ask tradesperson to contact them directly to arrange a convenient time.

Obviously, I then regularly check in with both parties on progress.

Guess what? The tradesperson usually attends very promptly. Could be luck but I'd like to think it's because we have a trusting relationship, and I pay them well/promptly, which I'm sure helps!

For one property, I've taken it a step further. I now ask the tenant to report issues direct to the tradesperson. I have a trusting relationship with my tenant and with the tradesperson.

We've built that up over the years. I cut myself out of the process, saving me time and stress. They keep me informed of issues, and any payments needed, but the day to day coordination logistics I no longer need to do. That to me is a prime example of how, with the right business mindset and systemisation, you can make life as a self-managing landlord stress-free, with minimal time spent.

Armed with this mindset and the above tips, you can easily deal with any type of repair or maintenance issue that pops up while your property is rented out. There's an endless list of issues that could arise, all requiring different specialist tradespeople.

You couldn't possibly be expected to understand or know about all these types of issues. I certainly don't. And the great thing is… that doesn't matter. The same process of asking basic questions, a small amount of research and then finding a recommended tradesperson who can resolve the issue for you works perfectly. And requires minimal time from you.

Finally, before we move on, in case you are wondering what some of the most common issues a landlord may encounter are, here's some classic examples, and how you can deal with them:

- **Damp:** Get extractor fans or dehumidifiers.
- **Pests:** No food left out. Get pest control in as a one-off.
- **Drainage issues:** Get water provider and/or plumber in.
- **Dripping taps/leaking pipes:** Plumber.
- **Boiler/heating issues:** Gas/electrical expert.
- **Keys not working:** Locksmith.
- **Blocked toilet/broken shower:** Plumber.
- **Problem neighbours:** Honest, open conversations. Police/council if those conversations don't go well.
- **Broken furniture:** Handyman

### 7.2.6 Get on Top of Your Finances

Before your finances get on top of you!

I'm going to admit, property finance is my specialist area. I love talking about it. I could literally write a whole book on it (one day, I will), showing you in detail how you can build the perfect process to firstly manage your finances, and then importantly analyse those finances to optimise your returns, which is accounting speak for "put more cash in your pocket".

I'm not going to do all of that here though, it would be excessive for the purpose of this book and section. Drop me a line if you do want to discuss it further!

Property finances are one of those things that most landlords shy away from.

*"Realising the need to submit an annual tax return, landlords often shove a bunch of crumpled receipts into their accountant's hands in January and hope for the best (and are then disappointed when the tax bill is higher than what they think it should be)."*

It really doesn't have to be, and shouldn't be like that. Use the same business mindset we've touched upon in this chapter: Systemisation.

Again, systemisation doesn't have to be fancy, even for finances.

How about this: Simply write down (preferably in a spreadsheet, website or system, but a piece of paper also works) each month what cash you have received, and what you have paid out.

Take it a step further. Can you categorise those cash flows? You choose the categories that work for you, but how about:

- Rent receipts.
- Mortgage payments (feeling fancy, why not split between capital and interest components? You'll thank me later).
- Service charge and ground rents.
- Insurance.
- Online agent fees.
- Repairs and maintenance.
- Other (i.e. utility bills).

Yet I don't want you to spend hours each month pulling together this list of cash flows. So, make it easy for yourself.

Use one bank account for all your rental property cash flows. Have rent paid to this account, pay all expenses out from the same account. Don't use that bank account for any personal items. That way, at the end of each month, you just need to scroll through the bank statement and record (or download) all the items from there.

I do this for six properties and it takes me less than 30 minutes a month.

Not only can you categorise the cash flows, but why not add a reference next to it? You can use this reference to refer to the invoice to which it relates.

Don't stop there though, why not add the location of where you store your invoices? These can be anywhere, either printed in a drawer, or in an email folder. Just put them somewhere consistent and note where they are.

*"I keep all my receipts in categorised email folders, so I always have them to hand on my phone if needed."*

Now, when it comes to the end of the tax year, you have all the required data in one place. You also have all the required support.

Your accountant will thank you greatly for making their life so much easier, and you might even be able to use this to negotiate your fees down.

Going into detail on tax and the tax return are also outside the scope of this book.

Instead, I just want to make sure you are aware that there are many legal ways you can reduce your property tax bill. One for us to discuss offline, or at the very least do some online research or speak with your accountant. Make sure you are not paying more than you have to!

And finally, for those who, like me, just love the new property finance data you are now in possession of, why not analyse your data? How profitable is your property compared to how much you have invested? What are your spending trends and how can these be reduced? So many metrics, so many ways to make more money. Worth a look.

As I said before, property finances are my specialist area. I'd be very happy to discuss with you some of the ways you can analyse your property data to make sure you are receiving as much cash as you possibly can from your property. Do get in touch!

### 7.2.7 Get a Frickin' Diary

After reading some of the above sections, you will no doubt be thinking, I need to have a property rental specific diary, or improve the one or process I currently have.

But really, a diary deserves its own sub-section when it comes to systemisation, such is the importance of ensuring you keep on track of the many different dates to save your lovely brain having to worry about these things, and of course, to ensure you don't miss any important deadlines:

Here's a list of the key uses of a property diary (in no particular order):

Useful diary reminders

- Tenancy agreement renewal date.
- Rent payments due.
- Legal documents expiry (EPC, EICR, gas certificate, etc.).
- Insurance renewal date.
- Tenant viewings.
- Handymen/cleaners/inventory clerk appointments.
- Mortgage expiry.
- Tax return submission deadline.
- Other cash inflows/outflows.
- Magazine/NRLA subscription renewals.
- Property group meet-ups.
- Property visits.
- Monthly/quarterly finances preparation.
- Goal setting and self-check-in reminders (covered shortly).

And remember, it's not enough to just add the expiry date for some of these items. What's the point in opening your diary today and realising your landlord insurance expires today? Wouldn't give you much time to quickly hunt around for a renewal quote. You need to add reminders in advance of the deadline.

You also need to adopt the mentality of checking your diary on a regular basis, or even better, have alerts that prompt you!

### 7.2.8 Store Documents Efficiently

If I gave you 30 seconds, could you find the EPC for your rental property? What about the title deeds?

It's not every day we need to use the legal documents for our rental properties. But when we do, it can be an almighty struggle to find them if we don't have a way of storing these efficiently. That struggle can be quite stressful.

Why not reduce that stress and unnecessary time and implement a system such that all the relevant documents, for each of your rental properties are in one easily accessible place?

I don't care where that place is. Printed out and placed in a categorised drawer, in folders on your laptop, in email folders, or in a fancy online storage app or website. As long as you know where they are, and can easily access them, that works.

*"I use my laptop. I have separate folders for each rental property. Within these, I have sub-folders for each of the different types of documents. I then also email each document to myself so I always have a copy on my phone in case I need it urgently when I don't have my laptop on me."*

What sort of documents am I referring to? There's a lot of them, but some of the key ones include:

- Title deeds
- NHBC certificate (if relevant)
- Lease agreement (if leasehold)
- Insurance documents
- EPC/EICR/Gas certificate
- Tenancy agreements
- Inventory (check-in/out)
- Deposit registration certificate
- Floorplan
- How to rent guide
- Photos/description for advertising
- Mortgage offer letter
- Property guide
- Bank statements
- Expense invoices
- Tax returns
- Passport & proof of address (always useful!)

### 7.2.9 To Do List

You now know exactly where you store all your contacts, referencing and documents. You've got a diary with reminders set for all key dates. You must be feeling chuffed at how efficient you are.

Well, why not take it a step further (I keep saying that, don't I?!), and have a specific property rental "to do" list? Simple concept yet really important in ensuring you work as efficiently as possible.

I'd suggest you don't combine this with usual household or separate work "to do" lists. Your property is a separate business, and therefore, deserves its own list.

Even if you manage just the one property, these "to do" lists are super handy for making sure you not only track what you need to complete, but also what tasks you have completed. The latter is useful to see where you spend time, to see how you could optimise your time spent in the future.

For example, if you can see you have ticked off five tasks in the last one month relating to "answer tenants' question on XYZ", it may mean you need to look at how they are contacting you, and look to change this (i.e. could they be asked to batch questions and send at end of month, or be told to find ways to resolve themselves, or receive better upfront explanation from you?).

**Landlord pro tip:** You can categorise tasks according to their importance and urgency. You could also have a section for those pending input from other people. These can be added to an app, or one of the many websites available or just in the notes section of your phone.

Or you can simply write them down on a piece of paper and tick them off with a good old-fashioned pencil.

How you do it is up to you. Just make sure you keep a "to do" list for your rental properties to help you be as efficient as possible.

### 7.2.10 Goal Setting & Self-Check-In

Arguably this final recommended system should be first in terms of priorities. Yet it is probably the one done least.

As a business owner, you should have a plan. Let's call them goals. And you should regularly check in on the status of these, along with your own thoughts on how things are going.

Important stuff.

Yet I've deliberately not added this section to the front of the chapter as there are plenty of other books, courses and websites out there that cover goal setting. These will walk you through the SMART goal setting concept (google it, it basically makes sure you set "good" goals) to make sure the goals are right for you and help you determine your "why" you own and run this rental property.

This book is about switching to self-managing your rental property, and this section specifically about systemisation.

So, from that perspective, it's simple. You need to:

- Set yourself goals (as only business owner should/would do). Keep them short and simple.
- Regularly check the status of your goals, and amend as necessary.
- An important third part I'd recommend is self-check-in. Yes, you may be on target to complete your goals, but how are you feeling along the journey? Yes, goals are important, but health and happiness are more so. So, make sure you check in with your emotions, and feel empowered to change your goals or approach if need be.

All the above items should be recorded in an easy to access place (see documents section earlier) with key dates and reminders diarised (see diary section earlier).

It's time to bust a myth…

> Myth: "I'm not organised enough to deal with all the admin of self-managing my property."
>
> BUSTED!
>
> Such a common doubt that landlords have before they switch to self-managing. However, this section on systemisation has shown you just how easy it is to implement systems that save you a lot of time and make your landlord life so much easier (even if don't think of yourself as being naturally organised!).

## 7.3 Getting Help

Being a landlord can feel lonely at times. It sometimes feels like you are having to shoulder so many burdens. But it doesn't have to be that way. In fact, with a little effort and a bit of networking, you'll never feel alone again.

Having a landlord support network, good sources of property information or even just fellow landlord friends to share stories with will make your journey so much more enjoyable, even in more challenging times. It's also the best way of keeping up to date with changing rules and best practices. This is essential reading for a smooth self-managing landlord journey.

I've listed out some of the ways you can get help as you go through your landlord journey. There's plenty more out there, and each of you will have your own preferences on how you connect with others or gain information.

### 7.3.1 National Residential Landlord Association ("NRLA")

NRLA are the best. If you do one thing as a landlord, it should be to purchase an annual NRLA membership:

*https://www.nrla.org.uk/join*

It's fantastic value for money at £75 per year at the time of writing (which is tax-deductible) and offers a whole host of useful information and support for landlords, including (copied from their website as I couldn't possibly word it any better than they have):

- Expert telephone and online advice from real people.
- Free tenancy agreements.
- All the documents, forms and guides you need.
- A 10% discount on Tradepoint/B&Q purchases.
- Extra discounts on services and products.
- News, videos, webinars and an exclusive magazine.
- Campaigning in government.
- Protection through Tax Investigation Insurance.
- Discounts on specialist training and accreditation.
- Extensive guidance around COVID-19 issues.

*"With NRLA coverage, you will sleep so much easier at night knowing you have the support and content from the best group out there. Do not skimp on this."*

They also do fantastic work on your behalf in terms of lobbying government to protect landlords' interests, promoting best practices (which is good for everyone), and helping change the public perception of landlords with media appearances and communications. Go them.

### 7.3.2 Support Groups

I imagine you find property interesting and like talking about it. You sorta need a bit of that to be a landlord, or you are probably in the wrong game. Well, imagine if there were groups, or places where you could go and talk about property to people who were also interested in property. That would be pretty cool.

Luckily, there are plenty of those. Let's start with online groups.

Facebook is the biggie, obviously, although other websites do exist. I'm in a number of property-related groups on Facebook, and I use these to get information, share information and enjoy feeling part of a group. Here's some I'm in that I find useful (many more exist, just search):

- *Landlord UK*
- *UK Landlords Support Group*
- *Buy To Let Property Group*
- *Landlord Tax*
- *Landlord Advice Network UK*
- *Property Tax Secrets*
- *UK Landlords Forum & Latest News*

A slight word of warning here. In large Facebook groups, you get all sorts (as you do in all walks of society!). So, not all comments are helpful, accurate or supportive. But by ignoring those few, you gain access to a wonderful group of landlords who provide some fantastic information and support. Get yourself signed up. They are free as well.

Then why not go a step further and meet other landlords in your local area in person? Even in COVID-19 times, there are loads of these happening all around the country, every month.

Here's a few meet-up groups to check if/when they are next running a meet-up in your local area:

- *Property Investor Network ("PIN")*
- *Progressive Property Network*
- *Premier Property Club*

There are many more, just google property meet-ups in your local area, then give it a go.

### 7.3.3 Other Sources of Information

It would be impossible for me to list out every landlord information source available. There are just so many! I'll list out a few that I use, and I'm sure as your property network expands, you'll be able to add to this:

**Your Property Network magazine ("YPN").** I love YPN and subscribe to their monthly magazine. It's stacked with useful information, real-life stories and ideas on how to grow a property business. Easy to read, with knowledgeable landlord writers. It's great value for money. Definitely worth signing up. Other magazines do exist as well!

**Property shows:** Want to send your landlord senses into overdrive? Why not attend a property show? There are many of these held around the country throughout the year (albeit, they have slowed in COVID-19 times). Here's a few I've attended and found useful:

- *National Landlord Investment Show*
- *The Property Investor Show*

**Property websites:** This is probably overkill, but you can also sign up to various property websites/blogs/forums where you can ask questions or follow trending topics. My favourites include:

- *www.propertyhawk.co.uk*.
- *www.property118.com*.
- *www.propertyweek.com*.
- *www.propertytribes.com*.
- *www.propertyinvestmentproject.co.uk*

**Property courses:** Lots of courses exist for landlords. The NRLA offer some great courses, which are worth having a look at. I'd start with them.

However, there are also a lot of expensive courses out there that won't give you any more information than what you can obtain for free online or by readying books.

If you do feel the need to sign up to a paid course, just make sure you do your research first to ensure they are reputable.

**Property books:** Of course, you are already reading the best landlord book available (as ranked by myself!). But if for some reason you hate everything that I have written and want something better, why not read a few other landlord books, which I'll begrudgingly admit are good (actually, VERY good):

- "How To Be A Landlord" by Rob Dix – this guy is awesome, I love his writing.
- Successful Property Letting" by David Lawrenson – he knows everything about being a landlord. Everything!

**Little old me:** If you really can't find the information or support you need from the above sources and are feeling desperate, you can always drop me a message! I love to chat property, and would be happy to share whatever knowledge I can.

It's time to bust a myth…

Myth: "I won't have anyone to ask for help if I need it."

BUSTED!

There is a huge variety of accessible information, numerous support networks and so much help available to landlords these days. You will never feel alone on your self-managing journey. The sky's the limit for how far you want to take it! Enjoy being a landlord.

## 7.4 Chapter Summary

- It's important to have a business mindset to reduce stress and allow you to focus on the big picture benefits that come with owning a rental property.
- Treat tenants as customers. This mentality can help you grow a long-term mutually beneficial relationship.
- Implementing systems is vital for any self-managing landlord to reduce time spent managing your rental property.
- Being a landlord doesn't have to be a lonely business. Sign up to and make use of the many outlets of information and sources of help available.

# 8.0 ENDING A TENANCY

All good things must come to an end. Or so the saying goes.

When it comes to property rental, this saying does apply in most cases: Your tenants will have been good tenants during the tenancy, paying their rent and taking care of the property. It's time for them to move on, for whatever reason, and you can use the simple steps in this chapter to ensure a smooth check-out while complying with the deposit return rules.

In other cases, you may decide to end a tenancy for what I'd call "good reasons". Need the cash for something else? Want to move back in perhaps? Rules to follow, obviously, but no reason why this has to be a complicated or unpleasant process when communicated and executed well.

Then there are the "bad reasons" for why a tenancy needs to be ended. Hopefully, you won't ever experience it, but as a landlord, it's a risk we all take when a tenant needs to be evicted for not complying with the terms of the contract (i.e. not paying rent, not leaving when the term is up, or other rule breaches such as anti-social behaviour).

It can get messy here. So, it's important to know what you can and should do here.

Again, hopefully not something you will encounter, but best be prepared just in case.

## 8.1 Your Tenant Hands in Notice – What to do Next?

In the vast majority of cases, a tenancy will end by the tenants providing the landlord with their "notice", i.e. saying they wish for their tenancy to end.

The form of this notification can vary, and will be based on the terms of the tenancy agreement. Usually requested in writing, but in modern times, an email or even text or WhatsApp message can suffice.

So, what do you do when you receive this?

Firstly, it's important to check if the notice provided complies with the terms of the tenancy agreement. If, for example, the tenant is three months into a 12-month fixed contract and wishes to leave within a months' time, that does not comply.

Let's say it doesn't comply, i.e. they wouldn't have met the minimum fixed-term of the tenancy agreement. You can decide how to proceed. You can reply back letting them know their request does not comply, and is therefore not possible.

However, you may wish to compromise, or even just agree to their request:

*"I'd argue that a tenant who wishes to leave but is not allowed to becomes a liability in terms of rent defaults or caring for the property, so I am much more likely to agree to requests like these."*

Again, in most cases, the notification will comply with the tenancy agreement. In which case, you can provide them confirmation (format up to you) that their notification has been received, and confirm the last day of their tenancy.

The important point when receiving "notice" is to communicate. Clear and regular communication will make the last few weeks or months of their tenancy so much easier.

Then you need to work through the below check-out items:

### 8.1.1 Tenant Communications

Prior to check-out, I liaise with the tenant on the following items:

- Agree with the tenant a day and time when they will check-out of the property. You may wish to arrange to meet them at the property at this time, but it's not required.
- Send a copy of the check-in inventory report to the tenant, advising them that you hope to return their deposit in full, and that the best chance of this happening is for them to ensure the property is in the same state as noted at check-in. This may include items such as:
    - Having the property professionally cleaned.
    - Returning the keys.
    - Making good any items broken or in disrepair.
- Advise the tenant to make arrangements to close accounts with utility providers.
- Remind the tenant they need to remove all their personal belongings, and that a charge will be deducted from their deposit for any items left behind.
- Ensure the tenant is clear on final rent payments, especially if a pro-rated monthly amount is required as part of the final payment.
- Ask the tenants to forward their post, and if they are comfortable doing so, provide you with their onward forwarding address in case.

- Ask the tenant what their preferences are regarding viewings for new prospective tenants, then do your best to fit around these.

### 8.1.2 Inventory Check-Out

Book an independent inventory clerk to attend the property as soon as the tenant has moved out. Try to use the same inventory clerk who did the check-in for consistency.

Word of advice on this. Think big picture in terms of maintenance issues or cleanliness of the property. There will likely be some items that will require fixing or cleaning by the tenant. You can wait for the tenant to leave and the inventory confirms this, or you can proactively have some of these items fixed at your own expense while the tenant is still there.

Yes, that will cost you extra money. But making the property good earlier will greatly enhance your chances of quickly re-letting the flat at a decent price with minimal void period, likely saving you a far greater sum of money. Don't get hung up on small things that a small amount of your cash can easily make good!

Keep communicating with the tenant in their final weeks, and give plenty of reminders on the above points to avoid any misunderstandings.

> Pro landlord tip: Once the tenants actually move out, I would strongly advise visiting the property yourself.

The inventory report will cover you for determining liability of any issues, but YOU, as the owner, should want to see the property yourself, to check a) everything is as expected, but also b) decide if there ' s anything additional you want to do to it. Remember, the period when no one is living in the property is by far the easiest time to get work done, regardless of whether it's picked up in the inventory report.

Make sure doors and windows are locked and the property is secure while it's empty. Taps should be turned off, bins emptied, neighbours notified. Not rocket science, just common sense items that you'd do if you lived there and were on holiday for a few weeks.

If the property is likely to be void for a longer period of time, you can likely apply for reduced council tax rates. You'll want to visit the property at some point to check all is ok, and it' s worth checking your insurance document that the void doesn't invalidate your insurance policy.

## 8.2 Deposit Return

Deposit return and/or deductions are always a contentious topic. They don't necessarily have to be though.

Here's an interesting fact for you:

*"A study by the leading tenant's website, The Tenants Voice, revealed that while 70% of deposits are returned in full, 17% are returned in part and 13% not returned at all. The survey of more than 2,000 private tenants also found that 35% of respondents had previously lost some or all of their tenancy deposit."*

Before we look at practical tips to make your life easier, let's start with the legalities of deposit return.

As a recap from the earlier chapter on deposit registration, you will almost certainly have collected a deposit of up to five weeks from your tenant, and registered it in one of the government-approved deposit schemes (custodial or insurance) and given a copy of the deposit prescribed information to the tenant. Good job.

### 8.2.1 Rules on Deposit Return

After the tenancy ends, you must return the tenant's deposit within 10 days of you agreeing how much they'll get back.

Simple rule, and should mean deposits are returned very quickly. Yet not so simple or quick when you scratch under the surface.

This is how everyone wants it to happen:

Assuming you are a good and pro-active landlord, you will have arranged for an inventory clerk to attend the property as soon as the tenancy ends.

Say it takes a few days to receive the inventory report, which you then quickly review and determine any deductions required.

These are sent to the tenant, who immediately agrees to your proposal.

You can then return the agreed amount, either paying this yourself (insured) or notifying the deposit provider to release (custodial).

A quick and easy process.

Everyone's happy.

In reality, there are many parts of this process that can cause delays, deductions or disputes.

Delays are the most likely issue. Unless you have not been organised in booking the appointment, the inventory report is unlikely to be delayed for more than a few days.

However, once received, there may be defects identified that require investigation to determine their replacement or repair cost. This is fairly common and can require you having to arrange for your local tradesperson to attend the property to give you a quote, which can take considerable time.

*"Once, despite my best efforts, it took me over three weeks to get a decent quote, which allowed me to make the correct and fair deduction from my tenants' deposit—all I could do during this time was ensure I communicated frequently and openly with the tenant to keep them updated on progress." (Christine, landlord)*

### 8.2.2 Practical Tips for Dealing with Deposit Returns

Once you have a reasonable feel for the cost of defects identified in the inventory report, the tenant may not agree to these—rightly or wrongly. There may be multiple rounds of negotiation, and multiple quotes requested from both parties to support proposed deductions.

Disputes and deductions do happen.

If they do, that is what the government-approved schemes are for. They provide an independent assessment of what amount of deposit should be returned. The scheme will ask you and the tenant to provide evidence to support your proposed deduction, which you can submit online. They will make a binding decision based on the evidence they have seen.

Try to avoid going to arbitration unless you really have to. I've been through the process a few times and it's painful as they can drag on for months. A quick agreement saves you and the tenant significant time and stress.

To help with this, here's my key practical tips I've learnt over the years:

- **Cover yourself:** Have an independent inventory report signed by yourself and the tenant at check-in and check-out. Keep receipts for expenses incurred and a record of communications.
- **Compromise is key!** Save everyone time and energy by trying to see from the tenants' viewpoint. Move towards that point as much as you can.
- **Be fair** (but firm where needed). As a landlord, you run a business, not a charity, so sometimes deductions will need to be made to recoup costs you will incur. Charge for those costs without guilt. But be fair. Don't charge more than you need to, and be grateful to the tenant for being a paying customer over the months—so give them some goodwill!
- **Don't quibble** over small amounts. Time vs money. Seriously, small amounts are not worth fighting over. Drop them, take the hit and move on. Stay sane.

This final point is key.

As a landlord, you have to focus on the bigger picture. Can't decide whether the cleaning cost should be £100 or £150? Honestly, go with the lower amount and make your life easier—short-term gains are not the main objective of being a landlord. You need a business mindset, one which focuses on the bigger long-term picture.

## 8.3 You Wish to End the Tenancy

This section will likely come with negative connotations. Your thoughts will initially jump to articles that will have been seen online or in the media about tenants not paying rent, destroying the property and then being almost impossible to get out of your property. You will probably dread this section!

Funnily enough, it was the last section I wrote—not planned that way but perhaps my unconscious bias of not focusing on a potential negative.

But why be negative when so many positives exist? Now, let me be clear, those unpleasant eviction situations can and do happen. But they really are the exception, rather than the norm. In the vast majority of cases, it is the tenant who provides notice that they wish to leave the property, and then do so in an orderly and decent manner.

When it's the landlord who wishes a tenant to leave, again, in most cases, this is done orderly and in a decent manner.

In a very small percentage of cases, things can get messy.

Regardless of whether your wish to end the tenancy goes smoothly (likely) or disastrously (unlikely), it's really important that you know the legal requirements of this process, as well as the available options for doing this correctly.

You must follow strict procedures if you want your tenants to leave your property.

You may be guilty of harassing or illegally evicting your tenants if you do not follow the correct procedures.

You can then use this legal knowledge (which is not that tricky), along with the steps and advice provided earlier in the check-out process and deposit return, to make a tenancy end at your request quite simple and pain-free.

Before I start on the legal rules, I'd point out two key points here:

- A whole book could be dedicated to this eviction section to cover every rule out there. This book is about helping you move to self-managing your property. Therefore, I' ll just focus on the key parts of the rules, rather than everything under the sun. Which leads me to the second point…
- If I could give you one tip about evicting tenants in these rare, messy situations, it would be to use the help of a professional. You can do it all yourself, but many companies exist that specialise in this process, and can help you get your ducks in a row—one mistake here can prove costly as you'll find out in a minute! Companies such as:

*https://www.ast-assistance.com/*

*https://www.landlordaction.co.uk/*

With that in mind, it's time to dive in.

### 8.3.1 The Rules on Evicting a Tenant

Let's start simple….

A landlord must have "grounds" for evicting a tenant. These grounds can be mandatory (i.e. fixed-term ending or rent arrears) or discretionary.

Mandatory grounds are by far the most common, as a judge must grant an order for possession if your paperwork is in order. Using discretionary grounds means it's up to the judge (as the name suggests).

> Under the Housing Act 1988, there are only two processes that can be used to end an AST agreement. They are Section 21 and Section 8.

I've added the link to the government guidance below:

*https://www.gov.uk/evicting-tenants/section-21-and-section-8-notices*

There are other eviction processes for different kinds of tenancies, but AST agreements are by far the most common, so let's focus on that.

Whether it's Section 8 or Section 21, the tenant must first be served a legal document known as 'notice'. It provides the landlord's grounds for seeking possession and tells the tenant that if they don't leave by a set date (at least 14 days after the notice is served), the landlord will apply to a court for possession.

*"Serving a notice quickly is a good way to show the tenant you are serious. Often, serving the notice is all you ever need to do."*

So, when to use Section 8 or Section 21?

Well, your situation might allow you to use either the Section 8 or Section 21 procedure, or it might force you to use one of them.

Under Section 21, a landlord is simply asking for the property back. They are not accusing the tenant of anything. The landlord must give the tenant a minimum of two months' notice and not require the tenant to leave before the end of the agreement or break period. That period was lengthened at the time of writing due to COVID-19, but will likely be back to normal now.

This is the most common type of how a landlord requests their property back from a tenant and, in most cases, is a smooth procedure, as long as the landlord has complied with all the tenancy regulations, has drafted the notice correctly and has served it correctly.

Here's where your newly learnt knowledge from the legal section of this book is CRUCIAL! Because… you cannot use a Section 21 notice if you have not given the tenants copies of the:

- Energy Performance Certificate – must be given before the tenants rented the property.
- Government's 'How to rent' guide – must be given before the tenants moved in.
- Current gas safety certificate (if gas is installed) – must be given before the tenants moved in.

Such important legal rules to comply with. And also so easy to comply with. No excuses!

Under Section 8, the landlord is asking for his property back on the grounds that the tenant has defaulted under the terms of the tenancy agreement. the most common include non-payment of rent, anti-social behaviour or causing damage to the property.

*"In most cases, particularly under Section 21, the tenant will leave when they are meant to (i.e. the set date per the notice)."*

However, if the tenant doesn' t go by the date on the notice, whether it's Section 8 or Section 21, landlords need to take the case to court to apply for a possession order. This can take about six weeks.

With a Section 21 notice, the tenant is not being accused of anything, so there is no court hearing. Instead, a judge simply reviews the papers submitted by the landlord and grants possession (assuming the paperwork is in order).

Under Section 8, as long as landlords can prove that the tenant has breached the tenancy, the court must grant the landlord possession.

If the possession order is granted, the court writes to the tenant to order them to leave. Usually, this is 14 days later, but may extend up to 42 days if eviction will cause the tenant exceptional hardship.

Normally, this is it. Very few tenants remain in the property after receiving a court order.

However, it is possible that a tenant doesn't leave even after receiving written instruction from a court, albeit very (very) infrequently.

In this situation, a bailiff can be instructed who will remove the tenant from the property, which obviously takes more time.

It all sounds very nasty. But remember, the messiest route really isn't that common. And the risk of this happening with you self-managing vs using a high street agent is no different. So, don't lose any sleep over it.

Time to bust a myth…

Myth: "I'm worried I won't be able to get tenants out of my property if I need to."

BUSTED!

You now know all the different permutations for when and how you can end a tenancy and remove tenants from your property. And it's generally a straightforward process.

In the rare cases where it gets a little messy, you know exactly where you stand, and how to deal with this on a practical level. Which is what matters. This worry is not something that should ever stop you from self-managing your property.

## 8.4 Chapter Summary

- Most tenancies end when the fixed-term expires, at the request of the tenant, and in a positive way.
- It's important to know the legal requirements around a tenants' deposit return, but also be aware of practical considerations that will make your life so much easier.
- In cases where you want a tenant to leave (eviction), there are two options available to landlords: Section 21 and Section 8 Notices.
- Eviction can be a long, messy process, but it doesn't have to be if you understand the steps and enlist the help of an expert.

# 9.0 OVER TO YOU

Well done for taking the time to read this book. You are ready to make the switch to self-managing landlord. It's time to ditch that high street agent.

Go for it!

Any misconceptions (the myths!) you would have had about whether you are able to self-manage your rental property have now been well and truly busted. You can smile a confident smile.

You know how to advertise your property online, screen and reference tenants, comply with all the legal requirements and prepare and manage your rental property throughout the tenancy. You also know how a tenancy can end. You even know some pro-landlord tips that will make you the best landlord around.

I wish you well on the next and exciting stage of your landlord journey. I'd love to hear how you get on, so do please drop me a message letting me know how it goes.

To set you nicely on your way, I've added a checklist that summarises each of the steps in this book needed to make the switch to self-managing landlord. Enjoy and get ticking.

*By following these checklist steps, you will have the tools and knowledge to confidently self-manage your rental property, earning you more money, reducing your stress and making you a better and happier landlord. Enjoy!*

## 9.1 The "Self-Managing" Landlord Checklist

**Steps <u>before</u> switching to self-managing:**

Calculate how much you can save by switching
Calculate the time you'd expect to spend by switching
Consider the other pros and cons of switching for YOU
Make the decision to "Ditch the High Street Agent"
Check contract terms with high street agent
Hand in notice to high street agent
Inform tenants of changes
Complete high street agent handover steps:

- Obtain their set of keys
- Ensure responsibility for utilities is transferred
- Clarify who will hold/register tenant deposit

**Steps to advertising your property online:**

Select an online agent
Sign up to the online agent package you require
Add basic property information to advert
Order photos and upload to advert
Write property description and add to advert
Get floorplan and add to advert
Calculate the cost of a void period for your property
Decide how much rent to charge
Select your viewing availability
Post online advert
Consider supplementary social media marketing

**Steps to choose tenants:**

Prescreen prospective tenants with short phone call
Give tenants regular upfront reminders of viewing slot
On the day:
    Arrive early, with keys
    Make property presentable
Negotiate offer terms with tenants
Select best offer online
Reference tenants

**Steps to ensure legal compliance:**

Agree terms of tenancy agreement
Collect and register tenants' deposit
Send prescribed deposit protection information to tenant
Legal obligations of a landlord:
    Obtain EPC and provide to tenant
    Obtain EICR and provide to tenant
    Obtain Gas certificate and provide to tenant
    Ensure furnishings are compliant
    Consider PAT testing
    Consider if Legionella assessment is required
    Review GDPR section for compliance
    Fit smoke and carbon monoxide alarms
    Ensure disability fairness
    Sense check property is fit for human habitation
    Provide tenant government "how to rent" guide
    Check tenant has a "right to rent"
Obtain permission (if required) from:
    Your lender

The local council
Your managing agent
Your freeholder (if property is leasehold)
Consider if you need a HMO licence
Obtain landlord insurance

**Steps to prepare the property for check-in:**

Consider if refurbishment works are required
Start building tradesperson contacts
Book an inventory
Get the property cleaned
Ensure you have enough keys
Update utility providers
Prepare a guide to the property
Provide tenant with your contact details
Ensure first months' upfront rent is received before check-in
Communicate with tenant on check-in timing
Consider welcome gift for tenant
Ensure physical right to rent check completed at check-in
Explain workings of property to tenant at check-in

**Key recommendations for ongoing property management:**

Diarise tenancy renewal date
Diarise planned property visits
Diarise dates of expected rent receipts
Store relevant property contact details and references
Store all property documents in organised manner
Set up property-specific "to do" list
Record monthly cash flows from property

Get property diary and add key dates and reminders
Diarise tax return submission date
Choose accountant to help submit your tax return
Set goals and reminders for status updates
Register with the NRLA
Sign up to property information sources
Consider joining online or local property groups

Printed in Great Britain
by Amazon

18685102R00129